AN EVENT-BASED SCIE...

OUTBREAK!

STUDENT EDITION

Russell G. Wright

DALE SEYMOUR PUBLICATIONS
Pearson Learning Group

MW01121428

The developers of Event-Based Science have been encouraged and supported at every step in the creative process by the superintendent and board of education of Montgomery County Public Schools, Rockville, Maryland (MCPS). The superintendent and board are committed to the systemic improvement of science instruction, grades preK–12. EBS is one of many projects undertaken to ensure the scientific literacy of all students.

The developers of *Outbreak!* pay special tribute to the editors, publisher, and reporters of *USA TODAY* and *NBC News*. Without their cooperation and support, the creation of this module would not have been possible.

Managing Editor: Catherine Anderson
Project Editor: Laura Marshall Alavosus
Production/Manufacturing Director: Janet Yearian
Production/Manufacturing Manager: Karen Edmonds
Production/Manufacturing: Roxanne Knoll
Design Manager: Jeff Kelly
Text and Cover Design: Frank Loose
Cover Photograph: Jean-Marc Bouju, AP/Wide World Photos

Dale Seymour Publications
An imprint of Pearson Learning
299 Jefferson Road; PO Box 480
Parsippany, NJ 07054
Cusomer Service: 1-800-321-3106
www.pearsonlearning.com

This material is based on work supported by the National Science Foundation under grant number ESI-9550498. Any opinions, findings, conclusions, or recommendations expressed in this publication are those of the Event-Based Science Institute, Inc. and do not necessarily reflect the views of the National Science Foundation.

Printed in the United States of America.
ISBN 0-131-66647-9
2 3 4 5 6 7 8 9 VG 06 05

1-800-321-3106
www.pearsonlearning.com

Contents

Preface

The Event-Based Science Model

Outbreak! is a module on diseases that follows the Event-Based Science (EBS) Instructional Model. You will watch television news stories about an outbreak of the deadly Ebola virus and read authentic newspaper accounts of the outbreak. Your discussions about the outbreak will show you and your teacher that you already know a lot about the life-science concepts involved in the event. Next, a real-world task puts you and your classmates in the roles of people who must use scientific knowledge and processes to solve a problem involving a disease outbreak in your community. You will probably need more information before you start the task. If you do, *Outbreak!* provides hands-on activities and a variety of reading materials to give you some of the background you need. About halfway through the module, you will be ready to begin the task. Your teacher will assign you a role to play and turn you and your team loose to complete the task. You will spend the rest of the time in this module working on that task.

Scientific Literacy

Today, a literate citizen is expected to know more than how to read, write, and do simple arithmetic. Today, literacy includes knowing how to analyze problems, ask critical questions, and explain events. A literate citizen must also be able to apply scientific knowledge and processes to new situations. Event-Based Science allows you to practice these skills by placing the study of science in a meaningful context.

Knowledge cannot be transferred to your mind from the mind of your teacher, or from the pages of a textbook. Nor can knowledge occur in isolation from the other things you know about

and have experienced in the real world. The Event-Based Science model is based on the idea that the best way to know something is to be actively engaged in it.

Therefore, the Event-Based Science model simulates real-life events and experiences to make your learning more authentic and memorable. First, the event is brought to life through television news coverage. Viewing the news allows you to be there "as it happened," and that is as close as you can get to actually experiencing the event. Second, by simulating the kinds of teamwork and problem solving that occur every day in our workplaces and communities, you will experience the roles that scientific knowledge and teamwork play in the lives of ordinary people. Thus *Outbreak!* is built around simulations of real-life events and experiences that dramatically affected people's lives and environments.

In an Event-Based Science classroom, you become the workers, your product is a solution to a real problem, and your teacher is your coach, guide, and advisor. You will be assessed on how you use scientific processes and concepts to solve problems and on the quality of your work.

One of the primary goals of the EBS project is to place the learning of science in a real-world context and to make scientific learning fun. You should not allow yourself to become too frustrated.

Student Resources

Outbreak! is unlike a regular textbook. An Event-Based Science module tells a story about a real event; it has real newspaper articles about the event and inserts that explain the scientific concepts involved in the event. It also contains science activities for you to conduct in your science class and interdisciplinary activities that you may do in math or social studies classes. In addition, an Event-Based Science module gives you and your classmates a real-world task to do. The task is always done by teams of students, with each team member performing a real-life role while completing an important part of the task. The task cannot be completed without you and everyone else on your team doing your parts. The team approach allows you to share your knowledge and strengths. It also helps you learn to work with a team in a real-world situation. Today, most professionals work in teams.

Interviews with people who actually serve in the roles you are playing are scattered throughout the Event-Based Science module. Middle school students who actually experienced the event tell their stories throughout the module too.

Since this module is unlike a regular textbook, you have much more flexibility in using it.

- You might read **The Story** of the event for enjoyment or to find clues that will help you tackle your part of the task.

- You might read the **Discovery Files** when you need help understanding something in the story or when you need help with the task.

- You might read all the **On the Job** features because you are curious about what professionals do or to find ideas that will help you complete the task.

- You might read the **In the News** features because they catch your eye, or as part of your search for information.

- You will probably read all the **Student Voices** features because they are interesting stories told by middle school students like yourself.

Outbreak! is also unlike regular textbooks in that the collection of resources found in it is not meant to be complete. You must find additional information from other sources too. Textbooks, encyclopedias, pamphlets, magazine and newspaper articles, videos, films, filmstrips, and people in your community are all potential sources of useful information. If you have access to the World Wide Web, you will want to visit the Event-Based Science home page (www.eventbasedscience.com), where you will find links to other sites around the world with information and people that will be very helpful to you. It is vital to your preparation as a scientifically literate citizen of the twenty-first century that you get used to finding information on your own.

The shape of a new form of science education is emerging, and the Event-Based Science Project is leading the way. We hope you enjoy your experience with this module as much as we enjoyed developing it.

—Russell G. Wright, Ed.D.
Project Director and Principal Author

Patient Zero

Hospital records identified him only as "Kimfumu," a 36-year-old medical worker. Kimfumu checked himself into the 350-bed clinic in Kikwit, Zaire (now called Republic of the Congo), in early April of 1995—a walk-in patient. Those were his last steps.

Kimfumu's symptoms were flu-like at first. He had a fever, an intense headache, and diarrhea—symptoms of a number of sicknesses. Hospital workers were not alarmed. In only hours, however, Kimfumu's condition worsened. Hospital aides noticed his skin starting to bruise, blister, and peel.

A few days later, Kimfumu was bleeding from every opening in his body. Blood oozed from his eyes, ears, and nose. He vomited dark, mushy matter, which turned out to be leftovers of his dissolving internal organs. Surgeons operated on Kimfumu April 9 and 10 to no avail. Kimfumu died four days later, but the mysterious disease did not die with him.

Nearly a dozen health-care workers who had attended Kimfumu soon suffered similar gruesome deaths, as did several Italian nuns who worked in the hospital. During the next several weeks, dozens of

---

IN THE NEWS

Ebola strikes Zaire's vulnerable heart

By Anita Manning
USA TODAY

KIKWIT, Zaire — The Ebola virus could hardly have chosen a more vulnerable country to strike than Zaire.

It is a place of almost unimaginable chaos, where the systems that make society function simply have crashed. That makes it a weakened prey for the devastating disease, which causes deterioration of internal organs and massive bleeding throughout the body.

For the people of this city of half a million, fear is a bright, sharp presence. "People are afraid," says Luck Nkiabo, a former teacher, now unemployed. "People are dying all over the city."

The emergence in Kikwit of Ebola virus, first seen in Zaire in 1976, became known when a lab technician died April 14. Other deaths followed, most of them among hospital staff who treated the lab technician.

But now, deaths are being counted in the city and the community, and many more are expected.

That a medical crisis of this kind would occur in Zaire is "not surprising," says World Vision vice president Andrew Natsios, "in terms of the massive deterioration of the medical care system over the last 10 years."

The economy is unraveling, he says, noting that per capita income in the country dropped from $750 in 1980 to $250 now. As a result, services normally provided by the government are non-existent or sporadic. Churches and relief agencies are struggling to take up the slack.

Doctors fear the Ebola outbreak, which has touched a handful of surrounding towns, will reach the capital city, Kinshasa, where nearly 5 million live in crowded squalor.

Families are crammed into storefronts that were shot up and deserted by owners during rioting by soldiers in September 1991, and January 1993. Taxi drivers skirt potholes that are five or six feet in diameter on streets that never saw pavement. Old men can be seen crouched on trash heaps, desperately looking for something that can be used or sold, while women, many with babies held fast to their backs with the same bright fabrics that make up their flowing dresses, carry bowls full of oranges or other foods for sale. Unemployment is said to be 85%.

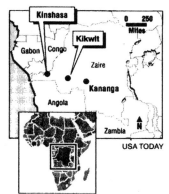
USA TODAY

About 300 miles east along the Kinshasa highway is the area of Kikwit, ground zero for the Ebola outbreak, where people live in homes made of mud brick with roofs of thatch or rusting tin.

Life in the city of Kikwit seems normal — crowds line the street and vendors sell fruit, fuel or other goods. But the talk everywhere is of "la malade" — the sickness.

A short drive up the road and past a cemetery marked by dozens of new graves, the hospital, a deteriorating tin-roofed building painted bright blue, stands behind a gate. Clusters of people stand silently at a safe distance, watching activity on the hospital grounds with frightened eyes.

Inside, iron beds line walls and masked hospital workers wash floors. At the beginning of the epidemic, local doctors and nursing sisters who have staffed the hospital for years cared for patients with a disease they didn't realize could — and would — so quickly turn on them. Now, only gloved and gowned doctors from the Centers for Disease Control, Doctors Without Borders, the Pasteur Institute and other agencies touch patients.

Despite a quarantine around the city, many residents of Kikwit are fleeing, using whatever modes of transportation they can. Many are bribing their way out.

Bribery is what makes things happen in Zaire.

Throughout the Cold War, the U.S. pumped huge amounts of money each year into the country's economy, helping to prop up the dictatorship of Mobutu Sese Seko. The greed and corruption of Mobutu, who assumed power in a bloodless CIA-backed coup in November 1965, is widely blamed for many of Zaire's current problems.

After the U.S. stopped sending military aid to Zaire in November 1990, things got worse.

"There was a gradual spiral into disintegration," says Hunter Farrell, coordinator for East and West Africa with the Presbyterian Church (USA).

Today, most state-run schools are closed because teachers aren't paid. Telephone communication is erratic at best.

Soldiers are paid about $5 a month, going months on end without any pay at all. They answer to whomever pays them.

Life expectancy in Zaire is short — an average of 52 years for men, 56 for women. Women have an average of more than six children each.

The state-run health care system is a disaster and people often put their faith in what Farrell calls "traditional practitioners who do work with varying degrees of effectiveness and hygiene, and lots of charlatans who put on a white coat and treat whoever they will."

AIDS is rampant throughout the country. Most blood banks closed a couple of years ago.

Medical supplies are scarce and nurses in state hospitals commonly demand payment from patients' family members before performing needed medical services.

USA TODAY, 18 MAY, 1995

people in Kikwit and surrounding areas succumbed to the mystery sickness.

Emergency medical teams rushed to Kikwit. Their first job was to stop the illness from spreading. Their second job was to identify the disease. They rushed blood samples from victims to the Centers for Disease Control and Prevention (CDC) in Atlanta, Georgia.

CDC teams work in four levels of biohazard containment. They base the level used on the deadliness of the organism. AIDS, for example, is classified as a level-three virus. Lab technicians at the CDC handled the Zaire blood samples with utmost care. They assumed the worst and assigned the samples to level four.

Each CDC worker wore total-body protective gear weighing 20 pounds. Filtered air hissing through these laboratory space suits lessened the chance that airborne contaminants from the samples would contact a technician's skin. It took several days to complete and verify the tests.

On May 11, the CDC issued its findings. Scientists had identified a thread-like germ in the blood samples from Kikwit. The germ warranted its level-four classification. It was the deadly Ebola virus.

Some researchers tagged Kimfumu as *patient zero*. He was the first person identified as contracting the disease in the 1995 Kikwit outbreak. However, evidence suggests someone from outside the city brought the infection to Kikwit.

A team of disease specialists traced the string of Ebola infections to an earlier source. A farmer and charcoal maker living just outside Kikwit became sick with Ebola-like symptoms on January 6. He died seven days later. By early March, a dozen members of the farmer's family had died. Investigators scoured the family's farmland for clues. They sampled plants, insects, and animals from swampy and forested areas. But the true source of the Ebola virus at Kikwit remained a puzzle.

On August 24, 1995, the World Health Organization (WHO) declared that the Ebola outbreak in Zaire had ended. The toll: 224 deaths in 315 confirmed cases. Approximately 71 percent of those infected by the virus died. Victims' ages ranged from 3 days to 71 years. The epidemic seemed to have burned itself out. No one knows why. However, the history of this disease suggests it will return.

Discussion Questions

1. What is a disease?

2. What causes diseases?

3. Can you catch the same disease twice?

4. How does your body fight diseases?

5. Where do new diseases come from?

STUDENT VOICES

During the outbreak, we washed fruits and vegetables with boiling water. We stayed at home.

I think the virus was in the monkeys around Kikwit.

Zairians eat monkeys, and I believe the sickness came from the monkeys.

RANIA AHMED
SUDANESE
KINSHASA, ZAIRE

On the Case

For the past few weeks, newspapers, radio, and television stations throughout your community have been reporting the spread of a serious disease. Everywhere you go, people talk about it. There have been several deaths, and new cases are cropping up every day. No one seems to know what this mysterious disease is, but it's spreading rapidly.

People are very worried. They want to know how to protect themselves, how to stop the disease's spread, and how to help the people already infected.

At a community meeting, each neighborhood agrees to develop a plan to protect itself. Your neighbors have selected four representatives who will look into the problem and make recommendations. You are one of the representatives!

You and your task team will research the disease and present your findings at a meeting five weeks from today. At that meeting, the mayor and city council will listen to the plans from all neighborhood committees. If they decide one plan is best, they will select it for the entire community. If all of the plans are equally good, the mayor and city council will recommend that each neighborhood continue to do what they are already doing.

Your Task

You and your team must determine what the disease is and how the disease is spreading. The Discovery File "Patient Profiles" contains medical reports on all patients in your community. Remember, they might not all have the same disease. Some might have different diseases with similar symptoms or test results. To solve the mystery, team members must perform their roles as described below. As a team, you will prepare a report for the mayor and city council.

Expert Roles

Read the descriptions of all the roles. Decide with your team which role best suits each of you. Make sure you are willing and able to meet the responsibilities of your role. Submit a list to your teacher with the names of the team members and their role

choices. Not only will your teammates be counting on you, so will the residents of your city.

Public Health Investigator
1. Keep a case log with the names of all suspected victims of the disease.
2. Include a map of the community that indicates where all affected people live and work.
3. Create a list of all events each infected person has recently attended.
4. Create a list of where each person has traveled on recent trips.
5. Create a list of family members who might also have contracted the disease.
6. Determine how the infected people are connected.
7. Decide how the infectious organism is transmitted to new victims. Then write a memo to health-care workers telling them how to protect themselves from the disease.

Physician
1. Create a log of all patients in the community. List all symptoms.
2. Record the results of all Science Activities.
3. Make a list or chart of all possible causes of the disease. Eliminate diseases as new information becomes available.
4. Once you know the organism causing the disease, develop a pamphlet to give your patients telling them how to protect their friends and families from the disease. You might want to add general information about preventing the spread of other types of diseases.

School Principal
1. Keep a school diary listing students who become infected with the disease. (You might add to this diary the names of students in your own school who become sick during this module.) Note whether other members of the same family have the disease.
2. List students, teachers, and other staff who come into contact with infected students and then contract the disease.

3. Work with the principals from other neighborhood committees to prepare an action plan for your school. In it, list steps you plan to take to protect your students and staff.
4. Develop an outline for a two-week unit on diseases.
5. Develop a policy for students and staff who show signs of the disease and state your policy in a memo.

Fast Food Restaurant Owner/Neighborhood Council Member

1. Develop a plan to prevent the spread of the disease among your restaurant workers and between your workers and customers.
2. Prepare a poster for the employee washroom with information on how to prevent spreading diseases.
3. Develop posters, pamphlets, and other components of a campaign to educate your customers about how diseases can be spread by the improper handling of food. The success of your business depends on its image as a safe place to eat.

Responsibilities of All Committee Members

1. The citizens of your community want answers to their questions. What is the disease? How can we prevent its spread to healthy people? How can we protect ourselves? How can we help the people who are already infected? Study any and all information you think is important. Conduct appropriate science experiments, read newspaper and magazine articles, and examine case studies. Use your creativity and the information you gather to prepare a presentation for the mayor and city council. Be able to support your answers and recommendations with sources and data.
2. Get a copy of the "Patient Profiles" from your teacher. Cut the profiles out and paste them on 3-by-5-inch cards. Arrange the cards in what you think might be a logical pattern showing how the disease spread. As you get new information, rearrange the cards.

3. Write a final report for the mayor and city council. Include your identification of the disease, a recommendation for treating the victims, and a recommendation for preventing further spread of the disease. Support your conclusions by referring to your research. Attach copies of supporting data to your report.
4. Develop graphic organizers (graphs, maps, concept maps, flow charts, grids, sequence maps, and so on) to show what you have found out and what you recommend. You will use these in your presentation to the mayor and council.
5. Decide as a team which one of you will say a few words of introduction, which two will give a short presentation of the report with visual graphics, and which one will close the presentation with a summary. Make sure the summary includes an explanation of your team's recommendations about how to deal with this disease.

When all presentations have been made to the mayor and city council, a discussion or debate will follow. You will help your class decide the best course of action to take.

The Contagious Town Meeting

Purpose

To generate a discussion of how diseases can be transmitted.

Materials

For each student:
- Disposable cup of unknown liquid
- Eyedropper

Background

You saw television news stories about the outbreak and rapid spread of the deadly Ebola virus. As with its earlier outbreaks, the Ebola disappeared almost as rapidly as it appeared.

You and your class might have experienced a disease outbreak too. The flu, or influenza (its real name), spreads quickly in a closed area such as a school. A student, unaware that the virus is multiplying within his red blood cells, brings it into the classroom. The flu virus escapes with a sneeze from the nose of its victim. It enters the bodies of other students sitting nearby.

The disease takes a while to show up. During this incubation period, the disease organism grows in numbers. Finally it multiplies enough that symptoms appear, such as fever and aches. By this time, the disease has probably spread to infect even more people.

After a few weeks, the flu goes away. How did you get it? Did you touch a desktop, pen, book, or backpack on which someone had coughed or sneezed? Did you touch an infected person directly? Did you share food or drink with a sick person? Were you in a closed room with an infected person?

This part of the activity shows you how a disease can spread through a population.

Imagine you are at a town meeting. You see people you know and stop to talk to them. One or more of them might be infected with the flu. They are contagious, but no one shows any symptoms yet. Do you have the flu? Will you get it?

Procedure

Caution: Some liquids used in this activity are poisonous. Do not taste any of the materials or get any on your face or skin. If any liquid accidentally spills on you, wash it off immediately with plenty of cold water.

1. Choose any cup and eyedropper from the distribution table. On a piece of paper, record the number on your cup. Each cup and its contents represents a person that might or might not have a disease.
2. Slowly walk around the room and occasionally stop to talk to someone at the meeting. Spend no more than five seconds talking to each person.
3. When the council president (your teacher) says "Exchange!," squirt four eyedroppers full of your liquid into the cup of the person you are talking with. Have that person do the same to your cup. Stir your mixture gently with the eyedropper.
4. Repeat steps 2 and 3 twice. Record the other person's cup number for each exchange. Do not exchange with the same person again.
5. After the third exchange, take your seat. The council president will add a drop of *indicator* to your cup. If you are infected, the clear liquid will change to pink or red.

Conclusion

1. Compare and contrast the results of this activity to the transmission of a real disease.
2. Work together to make a chart that tracks the disease as it was transmitted. Use the chart to determine the origin(s) of the disease.

Trying to stop scariest microbes

But 'with an outbreak like (Ebola) they should have their own airplanes'

By Kim Painter
USA TODAY

The first U.S. scientists on the scene of the Ebola virus outbreak in Zaire were determined to do everything possible to contain one of the scariest microbes on the planet.

That meant that two experts from the Centers for Disease Control and Prevention had to use their own gloved hands to scrub the bloody floors and remove the corpses the virus had left behind in its first terrible sweep through a tin-roofed Kikwit hospital.

"The hospital was a disaster," says Dr. C.J. Peters, helping to direct the operation from CDC headquarters in Atlanta. "I don't think there are very many people in the world who would have done what they did."

Says Dr. Frederick Murphy, a former CDC official: "It's heroic, going in there to work with Ebola."

"Heroes," "disease busters," "disease cowboys." The front-line scientists of the CDC hear it all the time. Their work is the stuff of books and movies.

But they do it in the real world.

And in that world, staffs are shrinking, labs are deteriorating and administrators worry about the day when two Ebola-like emergencies happen at the same time — and they find themselves short of heroes.

"If Ebola showed up in other parts of Africa now we'd be in trouble," says Dr. James Hughes, head of the CDC's infectious disease branch. "Or if there was a Lassa fever outbreak tomorrow in West Africa, we'd be unable to respond.

"These things don't tend to occur simultaneously.

"But someday they will."

At first glance, CDC seems fairly prosperous, an agency of 6,500 full-time employees, with an annual budget of more than $2 billion.

But a big chunk of that money goes right out CDC's doors to state and local health departments.

Other big pieces are devoted solely to AIDS, tuberculosis and vaccine programs. And in the agency's seven centers, researchers study everything from gun violence to birth defects to car accidents — an ever-expanding list that reflects a recently broadened focus on prevention.

The National Center for Infectious Diseases, home of the disease busters, has a $132 million piece of the pie. Its budget allows 965 full-time employees, and a two-year hiring freeze has just been lifted, Hughes says. But the center must cut jobs by 2% a year, as part of the government's downsizing program.

Still, the center's scientists and a cadre of about 40 public health trainees are expected to respond — in person — to about 70 infectious disease emergencies a year both here and overseas.

They call it epidemic aid — "epi-aid." And "it's the best job at the CDC ... where the action is," Hughes says.

When the plague hit India in 1994, an epi-aid team went.

When a mysterious respiratory illness started killing healthy young people in New Mexico two summers ago, a team was there within days.

And, in less than a week, their colleagues back in Atlanta identified the cause as a new hantavirus.

That lab work was done by the handful of scientists allowed to enter the CDC's own hot zone — the high-security, high-tech lab where workers wear space suits to handle the most lethal microbes — like Ebola.

It's the same lab where CDC scientists are analyzing Ebola samples sent from Kikwit.

Right now, only six people at CDC are qualified to work in the lab — which means that while the Ebola work goes on, virtually everything else screeches to a halt, Hughes says. He says he's busy recruiting and will soon have at least 10 scientists qualified to work in the lab.

The lab itself is a wonder of modern science, one of only two maximum-safety labs in the country and six in the world.

But the three buildings that contain the rest of CDC's labs are more like ancient wonders.

"If you stick your head into building 7, which deals with all other viral diseases, it's not nice. It's crowded. The air flow is inadequate. Stuff is piled in the hall," says Murphy, who left as head of the infectious disease center in 1991 and now is dean of the school of veterinary medicine at the University of California, Davis.

The working conditions are not just a morale hazard, he says.

"No one's going to die, but people can get sick."

He says two researchers in the old labs did die working with the organism that causes Rocky Mountain spotted fever in the mid-1970s. Poor facilities were thought partly to blame. That organism is now studied only in the new building.

But the viruses that cause colds, flus and polio, and the microbes that cause a host of sexually transmitted diseases, still are studied in shoddy buildings constructed in the late 1950s and early 1960s.

When he worked at CDC, Dr. Donald Francis says, "I was dealing with copper incubators that Louis Pasteur would have thrown out."

Francis worked on the first Ebola outbreak in 1976 and became famous for his AIDS work through the book and movie *And the Band Played On*.

He says finding money for on-scene disease investigations was sometimes next to impossible.

"I had to argue for every airplane ticket to go get blood specimens from the early AIDS patients," he says.

And he says nothing has changed. "It's all low-budget stuff, and I think it's a shame. With an outbreak like this (Ebola) they should have their own damned airplanes. ... If we need to send 40 experts over to Zaire we should be able to do it."

Those still at CDC aren't expecting such largesse anytime soon.

In fact, they're hoping they won't lose some of the money Congress has already promised for this year.

A pending bill at one point cut out $47 million the agency was promised for a new lab building. It also cut about half of the $5.3 million it was promised to invigorate its system for monitoring emerging infectious diseases — a system the CDC says needs $100 million to $125 million.

In the latest version of the bill, the money for the lab building and the emerging disease program is intact.

Meanwhile, members of the CDC's team in Zaire — three men, soon to be joined by at least one more — are doing their jobs.

One is in a village outside Kikwit, investigating reports of Ebola there, Peters says.

Another is helping to prepare several small clinics around Kikwit to receive Ebola victims now starting to show up all over the city.

And the third still is going into the ground-zero hospital every day to see bleeding, dying patients.

Peters says others in Atlanta are clamoring to go to Zaire and do exactly the same thing.

"It's what we do."

What Is a Disease?

Discomfort goes with being sick—you feel nauseous, feverish, stuffed up. A disease is a condition that impairs normal functioning of the body. The word is formed by adding the prefix *dis* to the word *ease*. A disease causes a lack of ease in your body.

Thousands of diseases affect humans. Infections cause most diseases. Organisms too small to be seen, called *microorganisms,* cause infections. The microorganisms that cause disease live in us, on us, and all around us. That's why washing your hands and maintaining other good hygiene habits is important.

Infections can occur within a single organ or they can involve your whole body. Sometimes they occur within one of the body's systems. A lung infection attacks your lungs. It reduces your ability to breathe and bring oxygen to your blood.

You and your team will be examining case studies of people sick with a disease. Most of these people will have respiratory disease symptoms. They could have tuberculosis, viral pneumonia, chronic malaria, lung fluke, or cryptococcus.

Diseases can affect any body system: respiratory, circulatory, digestive, excretory, immune, nervous, skeletal, muscular, reproductive, or endocrine. The endocrine system is responsible for controlling the body's chemical "messengers." It releases chemicals called hormones into the blood. Hormones control body growth and other changes in our bodies. Hormone-related diseases include diabetes, dwarfism, and gigantism.

An injury is a physical disturbance of the body. Although an injury is not a disease, it can become the site where an infection develops. Bacteria can infect a cut or bruise, and any germ can enter the body through a break in the skin.

The word *disease* is not used to describe the effects of aging. However, some conditions that are related to aging are considered diseases. Osteoporosis is a disease, for example.

Zaire outbreak is Ebola

By Anita Manning
USA TODAY

The mysterious and deadly Ebola virus has been found in blood samples taken from desperately ill people in Kikwit, Zaire.

The Centers for Disease Control in Atlanta confirmed the finding, says Ralph Henderson of the World Health Organization.

WHO and CDC experts arrived in Zaire Wednesday.

More than 100 people have died. The disease — transmitted through close body contact — causes fatal hemorrhaging, with blood coming out of the victims' ears, eyes and other orifices.

It kills up to 90% of its victims and there is no treatment or vaccine, says Dr. Peter Piot, who co-discovered the Ebola virus in 1976.

Zairean officials quarantined Kikwit, population 500,000, where the outbreak has been centered so far.

But Doctors Without Borders, an international group, reported 10 suspected cases in Mosango, near Kikwit.

The State Department is urging people to postpone traveling to Zaire.

But both the CDC and WHO say there's no need for concern outside of the central African nation.

USA TODAY, 11 MAY, 1995

Go Team, Go!

Purpose
To establish an identity for your neighborhood team.

Materials
For the team:
- 1 sheet of poster paper or butcher paper
- art supplies

Background
Community groups are often asked to present their ideas at town meetings. Sometimes, when the town is large, these groups create signs or banners to identify themselves. You have probably seen such signs and banners at political rallies, protest marches, amusement parks, and conventions.

Procedure
Get together with the other students on your task team. Invent a name for your neighborhood. Develop a banner or sign to identify your team. Be sure the sign has the following information on it:
- the name of your neighborhood
- a slogan or motto
- a logo that illustrates your motto
- the names of all members of your team

Now review the task with your team. Decide which role provides the best match with the skills of each team member. Your teacher is responsible for making the final role assignments but will listen to your preferences.

Design a standard form that all members of your team will use to keep notes during this module. This form will become a daily log. Include space on the log to write the following:
- what you already know about this and other diseases
- questions you need to answer to make the presentation
- answers to your questions
- ideas for the presentation

Conclusion
Bring this information to the first meeting of neighborhood task teams. Share your ideas and add to your notes any information you find useful.

McDonald's goes burgerless in Britain

By Shawn Pogatchnik
The Associated Press

LONDON — McDonald's dealt Britain's beef industry a severe blow Sunday by announcing it has stopped selling burgers. The move comes amid concern that "mad cow" disease could cause fatal brain illness in humans.

McDonald's, which serves 1.8 million customers a day at 660 restaurants in Britain, said it would not serve burgers in Britain until Thursday, when supplies of Dutch beef can be imported.

The nine Northern Ireland McDonald's and 25 in the Irish Republic will continue to sell Irish beef products, in which mad cow disease has never been detected, the chain said.

Britain announced Wednesday that scientists believe the cattle disease, formally known as bovine spongiform encephalopathy, is the most likely source of a new strain of a similar brain disease that struck 10 young Britons. Eight of them have died. A government report today could recommend slaughter of Britain's cattle herds.

Fears of the deadly disease have driven beef off many menus in Britain and badly damaged the $6 billion beef export market. At least 20 countries have banned British beef, including the two biggest markets, France and Italy. The U.S. Agriculture Department has banned imports of British beef since 1989.

"This is about public confidence," said Paul Preston, president of the British arms of the U.S.-owned company, which spends $37.5 million a year on British beef. "People are not feeling confident right now."

Public fear was reflected in newspaper headlines that screamed "DON'T EAT BEEF!" Sales of pork, lamb and even ostrich were up.

But evening guests at Simpson's-in-the-Strand, where Charles Dickens and King George IV once dined, weren't about to be stampeded away from savoring British beef.

"This is true Dunkirk spirit. We will pluck victory from the jaws of defeat," said manager Brian Clivaz.

An American couple out for their final night on vacation agreed.

"If we go mad on the flight home," Loretta Romao said, "we'll phone you." Said her husband: "Moo."

USA TODAY, 25 MARCH, 1996

Infectious Diseases

An infectious disease results when germs invade the body and multiply rapidly. They are transmitted from one living organism to another. Infection can transmit to you if you touch infected people or germ-covered objects, inhale germ-carrying droplets, or sometimes if you eat food or drink liquid that contains the germs.

A healthy person or animal can carry disease. Carriers do not usually have noticeable symptoms. For example, carriers can spread tuberculosis and amoebic dysentery.

When infective amoebas are swallowed or breathed, the single-celled protozoans take up residence in the intestines. Though microscopic in size, they cause very unpleasant symptoms, including diarrhea. Some people host the amoebas without becoming ill and pass the germs in their feces. In places with poor sanitary conditions, infected feces can contaminate drinking water or blow in the wind when dry.

In the United States, certain infectious diseases must be reported to health officials. Statistics on diseases are compiled at county, state, and federal health offices. This information helps prevent the spread of these diseases.

The list of diseases varies for different countries. The reportable infectious disease list in the United States includes AIDS, cholera, diphtheria, dysentery, Ebola, food poisoning, infective jaundice, malaria, measles, poliomyelitis, smallpox, tuberculosis, typhoid, venereal diseases, and whooping cough.

Germs that cause infectious diseases include viruses, rickettsia, bacteria, fungi, protozoans, and parasites.

Viral Diseases

Viruses are microscopic *pathogenic* (disease-causing) agents. They are on the borderline between living organisms and nonliving organic substances.

All other living things carry out nine life processes: growth, nutrition, metabolism, reproduction, transport, respiration, synthesis and assimilation, excretion, and regulation. Viruses on their own show none of these signs of life. They survive only by invading the living cells of a host. However, once they have taken over a cell, they control all its life processes.

Viruses cause diseases such as viral pneumonia, influenza (flu), rhinovirus (the common cold), measles, rubella (German measles), mumps, chicken pox, hepatitis, herpes, polio, rabies, warts, Ebola, and Marburg.

AIDS (acquired immune deficiency syndrome) is caused by a virus that attacks certain white blood cells. AIDS makes the body's immune system stop working. Without the immune system, the body cannot fend off serious illnesses such as cancer and pneumonia.

You cannot catch AIDS through casual contact. It is usually spread through sexual contact, either homosexual or heterosexual, or when someone uses a drug-injecting needle that someone with AIDS already used. In the past, some people contracted AIDS through blood transfusions. The blood supply is now carefully checked to prevent contamination.

Rickettsial Diseases

Rickettsia are microscopic organisms. They are bigger than viruses, which are very small, but a little smaller than bacteria. Like viruses, rickettsia do not grow outside living cells. Fleas, lice, mites, ticks, and spiders carry these germs. Rickettsial diseases include Lyme disease, Rocky Mountain spotted fever, and typhus.

Bacterial Diseases

Bacteria are tiny, single-celled organisms shaped like a rod, sphere, or spiral. Most bacteria are harmless. Some are even helpful. But the bacteria that cause diseases can be deadly, especially if the disease goes untreated. Bacterial diseases include some sore throats (strep throat), scarlet fever, tetanus, typhoid, diphtheria, tuberculosis, bacterial pneumonia, several sexually transmitted diseases (including syphilis and gonorrhea), leprosy, bubonic plague, botulism, bacillary dysentery, and boils.

Fungal Diseases

Fungi are classified in a biological kingdom by themselves. They can be parasites or harmless decomposers of dead matter. Like other parasites that cause disease, they live in or on other living organisms, contributing nothing to their hosts.

Some fungi grow in the hair, nails, and skin. Other kinds can grow in internal organs and interfere with bodily functions. Some fungi destroy the tissue of the host. Others release toxins (poisons) into the body, and the toxins cause disease.

Fungal diseases include athlete's foot, thrush (in infants), yeast infections, Tuck's disease, ringworm, and infection by *Cryptococcus neoformans*.

Protozoan-Caused Diseases

Protozoans are microscopic animal-like members of the kingdom of single-celled organisms called *Protista*. The name *Protozoa* means "primitive animals." Protozoans are almost as widely distributed as bacteria.

Most protozoans are free living and not harmful to humans, but disease-causing protozoans can produce serious health problems. Diseases caused by protozoans include malaria, amoebic dysentery, and sleeping sickness.

Parasitic Worm Diseases

Flukes are parasitic worms that can be found in human lungs and other organs of the body. Tapeworms attach themselves inside the intestines. Some tapeworm species can grow to more than 10 meters in length. Parasitic worms include flukes, hookworms, pinworms, and tapeworms.

Deadly virus's cause, cure puzzle scientists

Doctor Ralph Henderson, assistant director-general of the World Health Organization in Geneva, is involved in international efforts to diagnose and contain the spread of the deadly Ebola (Pronounced: EE-bola) virus outbreak in Kikwit, Zaire. According to Henderson, here's what's known about the mysterious virus:

Q. What exactly is the Ebola virus?

A. It is one of a group of viruses that cause hemorrhagic fever, characterized by massive internal bleeding. After an incubation period ranging from two to 21 days, symptoms start with a sudden fever and headache. The disease leads to bloody vomiting and diarrhea, bleeding from the nose and gums, pain and mental stupor or disorientation. Death may occur within 10 days.

Q. How is it treated?

A. There is no treatment, but in past epidemics, people who have survived have produced antibodies, the rest died and the virus ceased to spread. It may be possible to extract serum from survivors and use it to help treat victims with newly acquired disease.

Q. Where did it come from?

A. No one knows how or why humans get it. Scientists have examined rats, monkeys, bats and dozens of other creatures, but have yet to find the reservoir for the virus. Given that scientists don't know where it comes from, it's difficult to predict where it will happen next.

Q. When and where has it occurred in the past?

A. It was first recognized in outbreaks in Zaire and Sudan in 1976 and again in Sudan in 1979. It's named for the area of Zaire where it was first seen. A total of 500 people were infected in those outbreaks and 80% died. Since then, there have been no outbreaks.

But in 1989, a strain of Ebola virus was detected in monkeys imported to Reston, Va., from the Philippines. Human handlers developed antibodies to the virus, but they did not develop symptoms of illness.

Q. How contagious is it?

A. It appears to require "prolonged, intimate contact" with a person who is ill. In previous epidemics, cases have involved medical personnel or family members who cared for sick people and were exposed to coughing, or blood, feces or other body fluids.

Q. Is anybody studying the virus to find a cure?

A. Yes, but it is a very rare disease, killing hundreds or thousands, at most, and must compete for research funds with diseases like tuberculosis that kill millions each year. Public panic is not warranted. You have to work hard to get this disease.

— *Anita Manning*
USA TODAY

USA TODAY, 11 MAY, 1995

Doctor of Infectious Diseases

DR. WAYNE GREAVES
HOWARD UNIVERSITY
WASHINGTON, D.C.

In my youth, I was interested in science and why things work the way they do. Biology and the whole concept of life fascinated me. Why did animals live and why did they die? Some of my first encounters with biology were in a laboratory dissecting frogs and earthworms. It was extremely interesting.

My father, who was a funeral director, supported and encouraged me to seek a career in medicine. I grew up on Barbados, an island in the Caribbean Sea. We didn't have adequate medical services or doctors. People couldn't get the kinds of care that are available in the United States. So I decided to care for people who were poor and suffering. I entered the fields of science and medicine to serve humanity rather than to make money.

I earned my undergraduate degree in psychology from McGill University. In addition to psychology classes, I took science courses such as physiology, biochemistry, and genetics. I learned how the brain works. This is the scientific approach to psychology. After receiving my psychology degree, I went to medical school at McGill. I practiced internal medicine in Canada. Then I moved to the United States to study infectious diseases at Vanderbilt National University in Nashville, Tennessee.

One of my first jobs was working for the Centers for Disease Control (CDC) in Atlanta, Georgia. I was there for about four years as a visiting scientist. My time was spent in epidemiology (the study of epidemic diseases), public health, and immunization. I also worked with vaccine-preventable diseases such as rubella and measles.

Today I teach medical students and doctors at Howard University. Other doctors refer patients with infectious diseases to me. They might have something as common as influenza (the flu) or as serious as meningitis—a serious infection that can be caused by a virus or bacteria. Some of the diseases my patients have include AIDS, bacterial pneumonia, viral pneumonia, and Rocky Mountain spotted fever. Some patients have infections of the bone,

skin, or soft tissues. I also do research on the AIDS virus.

My days are very busy. In the morning, I meet with the infectious disease team. It consists of graduate medical students who are learning about infectious diseases and usually one or two medical residents who are training in internal medicine. We review the list of patients, and I assign them to see different patients. In the afternoon, we make our rounds and visit the patients together. I take time to make points about each patient.

We identify each patient's symptoms and discuss how the different diseases are spread. Questions include: Where did the patient contract the disease? Has the person traveled anywhere? How many cases are there? Should we notify the health department?

The health department can tell us if the disease is occurring elsewhere and what is being done there. Physicians everywhere report communicable diseases to help pinpoint outbreaks.

Sometimes we recommend tests that help make the diagnosis more specific. We also record our suggestions on each patient's medical chart. Private physicians are advised of our recommendations.

Our infectious disease team also visits the laboratory to review lab and culture reports. With meningitis patients, we examine spinal fluid looking for bacteria. We also check to see if glucose (blood sugar) levels are low.

With tuberculosis (TB), we study sputum smears. We stain the smears with a chemical that helps us identify whether or not the disease is tuberculosis. If results are positive, we start to treat the patient for TB and ask the lab for a more complete analysis. A complete tuberculosis analysis takes a long time—four weeks or more.

With malaria we look at a blood smear—a drop of the patient's blood spread on a glass slide. We check red blood cells under a microscope. If we find the malaria organism, we begin treatment.

At the radiology unit, we examine chest x-rays for evidence of pneumonia. People with pneumonia usually have bacterial pneumonia before they have viral pneumonia. In bacterial pneumonia, white-cell count in the blood is usually low rather than high.

Viral pneumonia is difficult to diagnose. The patient's blood sample is sent to the lab for a virus culture, but that can take quite a while. So we usually diagnose viral pneumonia by ruling out other diseases.

Some doctors like to treat every disease with antibiotics, but antibiotics can be harmful in viral pneumonia cases. Antibiotics do not cure virus infections. Our biggest problem is persuading doctors not to treat all infections with antibiotics.

Each patient suspected of having a communicable disease is assigned to a proper room. We follow special precautions so the disease does not spread. For example, if a patient has infectious diarrhea, we want that person to have a private room. We use the same procedure if a patient has chicken pox or bacterial meningitis.

Being an infectious disease specialist is very rewarding. It is not as demanding and strenuous as surgery. Yet it's very challenging. Collecting data, putting the pieces together, and drawing conclusions is really like being a detective. You have the satisfaction that comes from knowing that you can help most people.

If you want to be a doctor, biology is the most important subject to learn in high school. In college, study zoology, physiology, psychology, and other sciences.

Medicine, like all other fields, is moving towards using electronic journals and information. It's easier for me to go on the Internet with my computer and search the medical literature than to go to a library. Knowing how to use and find information on a computer is mandatory. One has to become computer literate to survive in the world of today and tomorrow.

Dangerous to your health

United Kingdom
1986 – Bovine spongiform
encephalopathy[2]
1988 – Salmonella enteritidis PT4

United States
1976 – Legionnaire's disease
1976 – Cryptosporidiosis[1]
1981 – AIDS
1982 – E.coli 0157:H7
1989 – Hepatitis C

Japan
1980 – Human T-
cell lymphotropic
virus 1

Korea
1977 – Hantavirus

1991 – Venezuelan
hemorrhagic fever

1994 – Brazilian
hemorrhagic fever

India
1992 – Vibrio
Cholera 0139

Zaire
1976 – Ebola
hemorrhagic
fever

Australia
1994 – Human
and equine
morbillivirus

The 10 biggest killers

355,000 Whooping cough
165,000 Roundworm and hookworm
500,000 Neonatal tetanus
1 million Measles
1 million HIV/AIDS
1.1 million Hepatitis
2.1 million Malaria

4.4 million Acute respiratory infections
3.1 million Diarrheal diseases
3.1 million Tuberculosis

1 – Water-borne parasite
that causes diarrhea
2 – Mad cow disease

Source: The World Health Report 1996

By Nick Galifianakis, USA TODAY

The rise and fall of infectious diseases

The World Health Report 1996 says approximately 52 million people died from all causes in 1995. Of these, more than 17 million were killed by infectious diseases.

Biggest killers were acute respiratory infections, including pneumonia; diarrheal diseases such as cholera, typhoid and dysentery; tuberculosis; and malaria.

Other major concerns outlined in the report, which is an annual publication produced by the World Health Organization on the state of global health:

▶ Drug-resistant strains of microbes that cause tuberculosis, malaria, cholera, diarrhea and pneumonia are having a deadly impact. Some bacteria are resistant to 10 different drugs. Resistant

bacteria are responsible for up to 60% of hospital-acquired infections in the USA.

▶ Cancer of the stomach, cervix and liver are associated with viruses and bacteria. More than 1.5 million of the 10 million new cancer cases a year could be avoided by preventing infections associated with them.

Some illnesses almost beaten

The good news: Progress is being made toward eradicating some diseases. Slated to join smallpox on the extinct list:

▶ Polio is targeted for global eradication by 2000. There are 145 countries free of the disease.

▶ Leprosy is steadily declining and "should no longer represent a significant

public health problem within the next few years," says the report.

▶ Guinea-worm disease, caused by a water-borne parasite that matures inside the body and escapes through a blister on the surface of the skin, could be eradicated within a few years. Cases have fallen from 3.5 million in 1986 to about 120,000 in 1995.

▶ River blindness, caused by a worm transmitted by flies, is being eradicated from 11 West African countries. The flies breed in fast-running streams. Blindness is caused by allergic reaction to the worms.

▶ Chagas disease, an insect-borne parasite that affects the heart, intestines and nervous system, is being eliminated from six South American countries.

USA TODAY, 21 MAY, 1996

Deadly History

The Marburg virus is similar in many ways to Ebola. In August of 1967, vervet monkeys captured in Uganda arrived in Marburg, Germany. A pharmaceutical manufacturer used the monkeys as test subjects for new vaccines. Handlers at the German facility went about their work preparing cell cultures from the monkeys' blood. They didn't know the monkeys were infected with an unknown virus.

Within days of the monkeys' arrival, 25 workers became sick. Although the disease at first resembled the flu, other symptoms quickly developed. Workers complained of rashes, diarrhea, and blood poisoning. By year's end, seven people died. Cases were reported in other European laboratories where workers were handling vervet monkeys from Uganda.

People who had no contact with the monkeys also caught the disease from coworkers. Is the vervet monkey the natural carrier for the Marburg virus?

Probably not! Because the monkeys died, the question remains unanswered.

The Ebola virus is more lethal than the Marburg. In July of 1976, a mysterious disease swept through Sudan in northeastern Africa. Two months later, it spread through northern Zaire, affecting the populations of 55 villages. In 1979, when the mystery sickness again hit Sudan, local doctors thought it was typhoid fever or malaria. Outside investigators later identified Ebola as the culprit.

The epidemic was named after the Ebola River, where the first outbreak occurred. (The Ebola River flows into the Mongala River, a branch of the Zaire River. Water that falls on huge rain forests drains into the Ebola River.) In these *hot zones*—areas contaminated by lethal, highly contagious organisms—hundreds of people died during the Ebola outbreaks. Close to 90 percent of those afflicted by the virus lost their lives.

STUDENT VOICES

When I came to school, people were talking about the Ebola outbreak. They said that when you get Ebola, you get blood coming out of your nose. They said not to touch anybody's blood, and not to eat stuff from Kikwit. I told my dad, "It's serious."

There were a lot of scary stories going around at school. Some of the kids were thinking they should go back to America. Then they were afraid that they couldn't go back to America, because the Americans wouldn't let people from Kinshasa come in.

During the outbreak, I was afraid to eat certain kinds of food, like salads, onions, and potatoes. I was only eating our own religious food, no hamburgers or things like that.

SIBTAIN BAWA
PAKISTANI
KINSHASA, ZAIRE

Chronic Malaria

Chronic malaria is an infectious disease of the blood. *Chronic* means it lasts for a long time. People who have a chronic disease often have it for life.

A parasitic protozoan causes malaria. The one-celled, disease-producing animal is named *Plasmodium*. Plasmodia have complex life cycles. Part of their life cycle takes place in a particular kind of mosquito. Another part requires humans.

In humans, plasmodia first invade liver cells. They reproduce in the liver. The new parasites are released to attack red blood cells. Every time a new batch of young plasmodia leaves the liver and invades the blood stream, the host feels symptoms.

Malaria causes fever, chills, and sweating. Infected humans usually feel these symptoms every two to three days. With some types of malaria, symptoms recur every few hours. A cough, diarrhea, breathing trouble, and headaches can also be symptoms. The loss of healthy red blood cells leads to anemia and its excessive tiredness.

Doctors use antibiotic drugs to treat malaria. As with the tuberculosis germ, some malaria parasites have become resistant to drugs. Researchers are working to develop new and different drugs to fight back.

Malaria is transmitted in the bite of a kind of *Anopheles* mosquito. This type of mosquito, and malaria, are mainly found in tropical and subtropical areas. One way to prevent malaria is to avoid areas with mosquitoes. If you are traveling in areas where malaria occurs, sleep surrounded by mosquito netting. Mosquitoes breed in standing water. Beware of containers and other places where rain water collects.

World travel to areas where the *Anopheles* mosquito lives has increased the spread of malaria. When examining your case studies, keep this in mind. Has the person recently traveled overseas? If so, malaria could be a main suspect.

STUDENT VOICES

When I heard about the Ebola outbreak on the 8 o'clock news, I was scared. They first said it was in Kinshasa, but it wasn't. It was really in Kikwit.

During the outbreak, we never really went outside. We were scared of the dust going into our eyes and noses. We washed our hands before every meal, and we were careful with what we ate. We stopped eating fruit, and stopped going to peoples' houses.

During the Ebola outbreak in Kikwit, I came down with malaria. At first, I thought I had Ebola.

GINETTE MUKOKA
ZAIRIAN
KINSHASA, ZAIRE

Flukes — What Are They?

A *fluke* is a kind of parasitic flatworm. Flukes can live in the human lungs, liver, intestines, or blood. They cause destruction and bleeding of the tissues where they live.

Flukes attack other animals, too, such as fish, amphibians, reptiles, and mammals.

Flukes are tropical parasites found mostly in the Far East. In some countries, they live in dogs, cats, sheep, and pigs, and in wild animals that eat meat.

Flukes can live *on* a host, but most flukes are internal parasites—they live inside the host.

The fluke holds onto its host by one or more suckers. It lives by sucking body fluids.

A fluke's life cycle requires hosts besides humans or other vertebrates (animals with backbones). Flukes also require intermediate hosts such as freshwater snails or crustaceans. Crustaceans are shellfish such as crayfish and crabs.

An animal or human acquires flukes either by eating the intermediate host raw or undercooked or by direct contact with young flukes. Mature flukes deposit their eggs inside the primary host's tissues. The eggs of many flukes leave the host through the digestive tract and feces. In humans, lung fluke eggs pass out in sputum.

Symptoms of lung fluke infection are similar to chronic bronchitis symptoms. They include coughing up blood, difficulty in breathing, and chest pain. Doctors treat fluke infection with drugs similar to antibiotics. These drugs are poisonous to the flukes.

To prevent infection by parasitic worms, avoid eating raw or undercooked meats of all kinds.

Long-gone malaria turns up again in U.S.

SAN FRANCISCO — Malaria, a disease wiped out in the U.S. in the late 1940s, is turning up again, say doctors reporting to the American Society of Microbiology meeting.

Three people in Houston who had not traveled abroad caught the mosquito-borne parasite in the summer of 1994, apparently in their own neighborhoods, says Dr. Ben J. Barnett of the Centers for Disease Control and Prevention.

The three patients, all men, lived within three miles of each other but had not been together, investigators say.

Investigators believe an unidentified person who had been infected with malaria in another country arrived in Houston and was bitten by one or more mosquitoes, and the mosquitoes passed the infection to the three men. Another 21 cases of malaria were found in Houston that summer, but all occurred in people who had traveled to countries where malaria exists.

In the 1990s, locally acquired malaria has been reported in California, Texas, New Jersey and New York.

"Most cases of locally acquired malaria in the U.S. occur where there is a high number of people traveling to areas (where malaria is common)," says Jeffrey Taylor of the Texas Department of Health.

The disease is probably underreported, Barnett says, and may be inadequately treated. He urges more careful reporting and treatment of the illness and more stringent mosquito-control measures.

— *Anita Manning*
USA TODAY

USA TODAY, 19 SEPTEMBER, 1995

Viruses mutate among underfed

By Anita Manning
USA TODAY

WASHINGTON — Malnourished people and animals may provide a breeding ground for dangerous mutant viruses that then can be passed along and cause illness in otherwise healthy people, scientists report today.

Scientists have long known that undernourished people are more susceptible than others to infection.

Today, at a meeting of the Federation of American Societies for Experimental Biology, researchers suggest there's a direct link between nutritional health and viral mutation.

Experts say the finding could help explain the emergence of new diseases from developing countries.

In research reported by virologist Dr. Melinda Beck of the University of North Carolina, mice deficient in selenium or vitamin E suffered greater heart damage when exposed to coxsackievirus, a common, usually harmless childhood virus that sometimes infects heart muscle. Well-nourished mice exposed to the virus were unaffected.

But, Beck says, when virus was taken from the heart-damaged mice and injected into the healthy mice, they, too, suffered heart muscle damage, indicating that the virus had mutated to a more virulent form in the malnourished mice.

The implication, she says, is that disease-causing viral mutations slip through the immune defenses of people or animals who are weakened by nutritional deficiency.

The mutants then replicate and can infect healthy people.

The finding is specific to coxsackievirus, but, "I'd be highly surprised if there weren't others" that react the same way, says virologist Dr. Stephen S. Morse of New York's Rockefeller University, an expert in infectious diseases.

If so, Dr. Orville A. Levander, a nutritionist with the U.S. Department of Agriculture, says the finding "could have public health implications.

"We are our brother's keeper," he says, "because we're not protected from what might be happening to malnourished people in Africa."

USA TODAY, 17 APRIL, 1996

Public Health Investigator

MARTHA BARTZEN
SAN DIEGO HEALTH SERVICES
SAN DIEGO, CALIFORNIA

I work in the community epidemiology office of San Diego Health Services. An epidemic is a sudden outbreak and rapid spread of an infectious disease. Epidemiology is the study of epidemics.

When I was young, I liked taking care of my younger brothers. I first became interested in a health-care career when I was in junior high school.

When I was 13, I was a "candy striper" at a hospital in San Diego. A candy striper is a volunteer who assists the hospital nursing staff. Being a candy striper allowed me to see what people actually did in a hospital.

Medical shows on television also caught my attention. I saw the excitement of working in a hospital and helping other people.

I also saw that there were very few Hispanic nurses in the community. There was a definite need for nurses who spoke Spanish. Being Hispanic, I thought I could also be helpful because of my understanding of the beliefs and customs of our culture.

After graduating from high school, I went into a one-year licensed practical nurse (LPN) program. If you are interested in a career in medicine or nursing, the LPN program might be a good choice for you.

After my studies, I worked as a nurse in a local hospital. Then I took a job at San Diego Health Services in the tuberculosis (TB) clinic. I gave patients TB skin tests. If a skin test was positive, we followed up with a chest x-ray. If the x-ray showed a lung problem, we called the patient back for a sputum test.

A sputum test is a check for active TB germs. (Sputum is the mucus and pus coughed up from deep within the chest.) Laboratory technicians smear a sample of sputum on a culture plate. If colonies of TB bacteria grow from the smear, the test is positive—the patient has TB.

When we're testing a patient for TB at the health clinic, we open the windows. TB is transmitted through the air, and we want the air to be circulating. Many patients with tuberculosis live in homes without good ventilation. Lack of good circulation and overcrowding promote the spread of tuberculosis from person to person.

If a student has a positive TB skin test, you want to check classmates by doing skin tests on them too. After someone is exposed to TB, it takes about three months for tests to show positive. If a test is negative, you go back in three months to test that person again.

If you're sick with an infectious disease, you can help prevent the spread. Always cover your mouth when you cough. Use a tissue if possible. Wash your hands often, especially before handling food.

Now my job is to investigate various diseases that are reported to health services. Sometimes I examine cases where people think they picked up a disease in a restaurant. Food-borne diseases include *E. coli,* hepatitis A, and salmonella.

Hepatitis A, for example, is a virus transmitted through feces. It's very important to make sure workers in restaurants don't have diarrhea and aren't preparing food while they are sick. If restaurant workers have hepatitis A and don't wash their hands well, the virus can end up on sandwiches, salads, or other uncooked food being prepared.

Our environmental health division sends inspectors to examine restaurants too. They place samples of food in labeled containers and send them to the laboratory for testing.

After the lab completes these studies, I talk to physicians about the case and make recommendations to the restaurant.

Right now I am investigating a hepatitis case involving four children. In trying to track the illness, I called each child's physician to see what tests had already been done. I asked the doctors what illnesses were being considered. From there, I started looking for an activity the children had in common. They might have all attended the same party or ridden on the same bus. It's frustrating when you can't find the common source of an illness.

Besides nurse, health service investigator, and inspector, there are other careers connected with fighting infectious diseases. For example, physicians oversee the work of nurses, investigators, and inspectors. Epidemiologists study communicable diseases. They explain trends in the data and help determine what to do about the problem.

If you are interested in a health-care career, work hard in science classes such as biology, chemistry, and health science. Take a course in anatomy and physiology if your school offers it. Doing well in these classes will make the courses you take in college much easier.

Ebola outbreak triggers terror

By Jack Kelley
and Chris Erasmus
USA TODAY

Villagers are torching their homes. Hospital patients are fleeing from their beds.

An outbreak of the deadly Ebola virus that has so far claimed more than 100 lives in Kikwit, Zaire, is sending shock waves worldwide.

"People are streaming in large numbers out of Kikwit and into the surrounding jungle to escape this outbreak," says doctor David Tembo, a World Health Organization official in Johannesburg.

Doctors went on the offensive Wednesday trying to calm a nervous public:

▶ "This is not a public health emergency," says Ralph Henderson, assistant director-general for the Geneva-based World Health Organization. "(It) can be stopped on a dime if we can just get in there and ... get things done."

▶ "This one is deadly, of course, but it's not infectious in the way that the plague or influenza is infectious. It's not airborne," says WHO spokesman Thomson Prentice.

Still, the Ebola virus — named after a north Zairean river where the first outbreak was reported in 1976 — may be spreading.

The international aid group Doctors Without Borders reports that at least 10 people in Mosango, 75 miles west of Kikwit, may also have been infected. Three of the 10 have died.

The Little Sisters of the Poor, an order of Catholic nuns based in Bergamo, Italy, says two sisters have died in the past two weeks in Kikwit. Two other members of the order, Sisters Danieangela Sorti, 48, and Dinarosa Belleri, 58, are in "stable but grave condition" at a Kikwit hospital, a statement says.

"What is worrying me and many others ... is that for every hour that goes by without having proper isolation procedures, the greater the chances that someone will transmit the infection to a major urban center in Africa, Europe or North America," Tembo says.

Recent media hype appears to be contributing to the growing concern, too.

Monday's NBC-TV movie *Robin Cook's Virus* and a best-selling book, *The Hot Zone* by Richard Preston, which focuses on an outbreak of the Ebola virus among monkeys outside Washington, are adding to concerns.

Additionally, the movie *Outbreak* released in March in the USA and now showing in Europe, tells the story of hundreds of people in a California town infected by a virus carried by a pet monkey from Zaire.

"I'm afraid this could be the next AIDS," says Stephen Olsen, 22, of Frankfurt, emerging from a German theater after watching the film. "It's going to spread quickly."

Still, nowhere is the fear as great as in central Africa.

"There are other missionaries in the area who are afraid," says an Italian missionary, Father Julio Albanesi of the Comboni Missionaries in Nairobi. "When you get it, in less than six days ... you die."

Adds Sister Maria Antonelli, a Jesuit nun based in Nairobi: "Our sisters have never prayed harder than since the Ebola broke out. First AIDS, now this."

Cryptococcus neoformans

Cryptococcus neoformans is a single-celled, yeastlike fungus that causes diseases in humans. It lives in soil, especially soil enriched with pigeon droppings. It is common in pigeon roosts and nests.

C. neoformans can infect the lungs, kidneys, prostate, and bones. Symptoms include a fever, cough, and thick yellow sputum that can contain blood in the most advanced cases.

This fungus can also cause a form of meningitis, which is inflammation of the tissues that cover the brain and spinal cord. This form of meningitis is more common in tropical and subtropical climates.

A person infected by C. neoformans might have skin with lesions, ulcers, or tumorlike masses. The disease affects males more than females. Five to ten percent of AIDS patients in the United States develop the disease. Infections can also occur in cats, dogs, horses, cows, monkeys, and other animals.

Removing large deposits of pigeon droppings and cleaning the area with a chemical disinfectant can help keep the fungus from spreading. Doctors use antibiotics to treat infected people.

Painful, flu-like tropical illness can be deadly

By Anita Manning
USA TODAY

Dengue fever, a tropical "flu" that health officials are calling a global pandemic, is raging through Central and South America and now threatens to fly on mosquito wings into the United States. Doctors with the Texas Department of Health found out last month that 200 to 300 cases of dengue (DEN-gay) and its murderous twin, dengue hemorrhagic fever, have occurred in Reynosa, a Mexican border town just over the line from McAllen, Texas.

Dengue fever spreads, hits Caribbean

By Anita Manning
USA TODAY

Reports of dengue fever and its more dangerous form, dengue hemorrhagic fever, have nearly doubled in two months throughout Central America, says the Pan American Health Organization.

The mosquito-borne disease also has spread into the Caribbean, threatening residents and the tourist economy.

A PAHO report calls the spread "an acute problem of serious proportions in the Americas. The situation has become a health and sociopolitical emergency."

Dengue hemorrhagic fever, or DHF, causes high fever, hemorrhage and shock. It kills up to 20% of victims. The milder form is similar to severe flu. While there is no vaccine or specific treatment, medical care to replace fluids can save lives. PAHO reports:

▶ Since September, the number of dengue cases in Central America increased from 23,603 to 46,532. During the same period, reports of DHF rose from 352 to 546.

▶ Jamaica has 228 confirmed cases of dengue, 800 suspected, and 22 of DHF. Cases have been reported in 13 other Caribbean countries.

Primarily a scourge of the tropics, dengue causes high fevers and severe achiness. There's no vaccine and no specific treatment beyond bed rest and fluids. "It's a bad, bad flu," says Dr. Leonel Vela of Harlingen, Texas, regional medical director for the state health department. In most cases, "it's not fatal, but you might wish it were. You don't want to get this."

USA TODAY, 18 SEPTEMBER, 1995

USA TODAY, 20 NOVEMBER, 1995

Viral Pneumonia

Pneumonia is an acute infection of the lungs in which the air sacs begin to fill with fluid. Dying from pneumonia is like drowning. *Acute* means the disease comes on quickly and has severe symptoms. Pneumonia can be caused by injury, a diplococcus (double sphere) bacteria, or any of several different viruses.

Viral pneumonia can occur by itself or at the same time as other diseases such as flu (influenza), measles, or chicken pox. Doctors did not recognize the viral form until the 1930s.

Viruses are extremely small. Scientists believe that a single virus particle can reproduce itself in a host cell. Viruses do not reproduce by growth and cell division as cells do. Instead, they cause the host cell to produce virus parts, which then assemble themselves into new viruses.

Symptoms of viral pneumonia include headache, fever, muscle pain, and a cough that produces a thick sputum. The patient makes a bubbling, crackling sound when breathing in and out. (A stethoscope can amplify this sound.) The bubbling sound is similar to what you hear when you blow air through a straw into a glass of water. The crackling resembles the noise made when you crumple a piece of paper or cellophane.

To guard against catching viral pneumonia and many other diseases, you should wash your hands frequently and never put your fingers directly in your eyes, nose, or mouth.

The only treatment for viral pneumonia is basic care for the infected person. Antibiotic drugs will not work against a virus. Doctors usually use antibiotics to fight infections caused by bacteria or fungi. A doctor might prescribe antibiotics if the person also has a bacterial infection, but there are no drugs to fight viruses.

I N   T H E   N E W S

Lyme-causing tick carries worse disease

SAN FRANCISCO — A newly discovered bacteria carried by the same tick that transmits Lyme disease may be far more common than previously known, researchers reported Monday.

Human Granulocytic Ehrlichiosis is a sometimes-fatal disease that causes high fever, headache, muscle aches or chills. Only about 150 cases have been identified, more than 90% of them in Wisconsin and Minnesota. But, say Dr. Johan S. Bakken of Duluth, Minn., and Dr. J. Stephen Dumler of the University of Maryland Medical Center, it's probably going undiagnosed in many patients.

"It is still emerging," says Bakken. "We're just discovering the tip of the iceberg."

Wherever there is Lyme disease, carried by the tiny deer tick, you likely will find HGE, says Dumler. "That has proven to be true so far," he says. The doctors presented findings here Monday to the American

> **66 We're just discovering the tip of the iceberg. 99**
>
> — Dr. Johan S. Bakken

Society for Microbiology.

HGE is known to have killed four people. The doctors believe HGE "alters the immune system," says Dumler, making people vulnerable to opportunistic infection.

Unlike Lyme disease, which responds to several antibiotics, HGE is sensitive only to tetracycline and doxycycline. Dumler and Bakken predict that about 10% of patients with Lyme disease also have HGE. They recommend that doctors put all Lyme disease patients on a two-week course of treatment with doxycycline.

— Anita Manning
USA TODAY

USA TODAY, 19 SEPTEMBER, 1995

Tuberculosis

Tuberculosis is an infectious disease that usually attacks the lungs. It can also infect other parts of the body. Tuberculosis is also called *TB* and *consumption*. Tuberculosis germs need oxygen to live. Like many other germs, they thrive in warm, moist, dark places. The lungs are a perfect location for TB germs.

The bacterium *Mycobacterium tuberculosis* causes TB. These germs cannot move on their own. They need a cough or sneeze to propel them into the air. People or animals inhale the germs and provide comfortable new homes for them. TB only grows and reproduces inside the body of a human or other animal (although scientists can grow TB in a laboratory).

What happens when a person inhales TB germs? First, the body's immune system goes into action. Phagocytes, a type of white blood cell, attack and kill many TB germs. Then other defending cells surround the surviving TB germs. Hard lumps, called *tubercles,* form during this stage. Tuberculosis was named for these lumps.

The disease can stay inside the tubercles for months or years, coming and going depending on the person's health. In some cases, infected people show no symptoms. They become carriers of the disease who can pass on the TB germs by coughing and sneezing.

People with active cases of TB can have fever, night sweats, and weight loss. They often cough up blood. Sometimes the germs spread from the lungs to the blood stream. Millions of tiny tubercles can form throughout the body.

TB can also enter the body through the milk of an infected cow. This happens only if the cow's health is not monitored and its milk is not pasteurized. Where health standards are low or people do not have access to medical care, TB spreads easily.

How do you prevent the spread of TB? First, you need to know who has it and who does not. TB skin tests, x-ray screenings, and laboratory tests of sputum (coughed-up mucus) are the diagnostic methods. You need all three to confirm a TB diagnosis. Testing just for the presence of TB antibodies will produce many false positive results. When a person is exposed to TB, they make antibodies against it, *whether or not the disease actually develops*. A positive TB test does not mean that a person has TB or has ever had TB. It only means that they have been exposed to it in the past.

When you are developing your community's disease prevention plan, remember that you will have a limited amount of money. You might have to decide whether to test everyone for TB or only people most likely infected.

Doctors today treat almost all TB infections with antibiotics, but scientists are worried. Some strains of TB are becoming resistant to antibiotics. The national Centers for Disease Control and Prevention (CDC) in Atlanta, Georgia, and other health research facilities are searching for new ways to combat these hardy germs.

Virus Carriers

In Zaire, the Ebola virus first appeared in 1976. Medical authorities were able to trace the deadly trail of the virus back to a point of origin—an infected man who entered a local clinic. The clinic lacked supplies and sanitary safeguards. The same medical items, such as syringes, used to treat the man were used on other patients.

As the 1995 outbreak claimed its victims, panic gripped the 500,000 residents of Kikwit. Symptoms reported were the same as those seen in the 1976 outbreak.

Government authorities closed schools and ordered residents to stay off the streets. Some residents set fire to their homes. People held handkerchiefs tightly over their noses and mouths as they darted through the city. Authorities ordered house-to-house checks to locate potential carriers. The reality that Ebola does not easily spread did not calm fears.

Ebola is typically fatal to 90 percent of those who contract the disease. Worse yet, the incubation period for Ebola can be as short as 3 or as long as 18 days. The virus usually kills its host swiftly. A quick death is a blessing in some ways. Ebola victims have little chance to transmit the disease to others.

Ebola can be transmitted only through contact with infected bodily fluids or blood. Sexual transmission of the virus is considered possible but unlikely because infected people quickly become too ill to participate in sexual activity. The virus cannot be spread through the air. The public largely ignored these facts as reports of Ebola-caused deaths mounted. Coffins pushed by people wearing protective garb became a common sight.

Many people worried day after day whether they harbored the virus. Some locked themselves in their homes awaiting the first, frightful symptoms of Ebola.

The Kikwit hospital emptied as workers and many patients fled. At times, armed soldiers stood guard outside the medical center's doors. In an effort to curb the disease's spread, they kept patients suffering from Ebola symptoms inside and kept their families outside. In several cases, families were stopped from providing their dead loved ones the customary ritual washing. Authorities feared the practice could spread the virus. Additional hospitals were named to isolate those infected with Ebola.

Kikwit was ground zero for the Ebola outbreak; the Zairian government imposed a quarantine on the city. The tactic proved unworkable. Roadblocks covered the main highway leaving Kikwit, but some people escaped anyway—on river boats and by aircraft. Neighboring countries tightened their border checks. The U.S. State Department urged people to delay any travel to Zaire. Several international airlines and airports began monitoring passengers from Zaire. Researchers combed nearby forest regions, trapping animals and insects they hoped might lead to the source of the virus.

Health officials went to neighboring Kinshasa, the capital of Zaire. They sought the whereabouts of people who could have transported Ebola to that city of four million. At one point, nearly two dozen foreign reporters covering the epidemic were quarantined for 28 days.

Ironically, newspaper accounts of the Ebola epidemic were matched by the release of the movie *Outbreak*. The fictional film tells the story of a California town threatened by a virus-carrying monkey from Zaire.

Could the Ebola virus ever reach the United States? It already has. In 1989, a shipment of monkeys from the Philippines arrived at a primate quarantine facility in Reston, Virginia. The animals were among the 16,000 wild monkeys imported each year into the United States for research.

Monkeys from tropical regions around the world are put in quarantine. After 30 days, they can be transported around the country. The month-long quarantine supposedly prevents diseases from spreading to other animals and to humans.

Within weeks of their arrival in Reston, nearly a third of the monkeys died. Scientists determined later that the primates carried a weaker strain of the Ebola virus—the Reston virus. Fortunately, humans infected with this strain typically ran a high fever but did not die.

The U.S. Army destroyed the monkeys, then decontaminated the holding facility. The entire quarantine building was ultimately leveled. Richard Preston documented the episode in the book *The Hot Zone* (Random House, New York, 1994). The incident spurred the Centers for Disease Control (CDC) to create stricter import regulations on monkeys.

Marburg, Ebola, and Reston diseases are now identified as members of the *Filoviridae,* a distinct family of viruses whose name comes from the germs' filamentlike shape. Where do these deadly viruses come from? No one knows for sure. More important, no one has identified a vaccine or treatment for Ebola.

STUDENT VOICES

I first heard about Ebola at school and from my father. We just heard that there was an outbreak in Kikwit and that it was killing many people. The first time we heard it, we didn't know it was Ebola. Somebody thought it was called *diarrhea fever* (a similar disease, but not as deadly).

My father was at a conference with other church members who had visited sick people in Kikwit. He was worried that they might bring it back to Kinshasa. My father also knew some church people in Kikwit.

We went on summer vacation to South Africa. When we crossed the border between South Africa and Botswana, they made us wait. They had to check us. We waited about three hours at the border, and then they took us to a hospital. We had to wait there for the doctor. When the doctor came, he was embarrassed. He knew that you can't tell if somebody has Ebola unless they are actually sick. So he let us go. At that point we were not worried about Ebola, but the people in Botswana were still worried.

KARINA DERKSEN
CANADIAN/AMERICAN
KINSHASA, ZAIRE

Diseases Throughout History

The fight against disease is a common theme in human history. Paleontologists and anthropologists have found evidence that diseases were rampant in ancient times. An Egyptian stone tablet from 1400 B.C. shows a man with a withered leg typical of polio. Skeletons of villagers in Denmark and Norway from 2,000 years ago show that they had rickets, which is caused by lack of vitamin D.

Smallpox flourished until recently. It was first recorded in ancient Egypt. Archaeologists found signs of a smallpox rash on the mummy of Ramses V who died in 1156 B.C. Smallpox has finally been eradicated. The last case was recorded in 1977 in Somalia, in eastern Africa.

In the winter of 1918–1919, influenza (flu) killed 21 million people throughout the world, about 500,000 of them in the United States alone.

Bubonic plague, or Black Death, has reappeared frequently throughout recorded time. During the third century, 5,000 people died every day during an outbreak of the plague in Athens. Then in 542 A.D., bubonic plague hit Constantinople, killing up to 10,000 a day. In the fourteenth century, the plague killed a third of all Europeans— about 25 million people.

The symptoms of bubonic plague include rapid pulse, fever, chest pain, coughing, vomiting blood, and painful swelling in the groin or armpits. No one knew what caused the plague or how it spread.

Then in 1894, Shibasaburo Kitasato in Japan and Alexandre Yersin in France each independently identified the bacterium that causes bubonic plague. In 1897, Robert Koch from Germany demonstrated that bubonic plague is carried by rats and spread by fleas. Because of such discoveries, bubonic plague is curable today. Researchers hope that similar discoveries about Ebola will lead to its cure as well.

Amtrak warns riders of possible TB risk

By Shannon Tangonan
USA TODAY

Health officials are warning about 400 Amtrak passengers that they should get tested for tuberculosis because a sick passenger may have exposed them to the disease.

The man "was coughing and he had mucus all over him," said passenger Maureen Reardon of New York City. He also spit up blood, which got on one other passenger, she said.

The 22-year-old man was in fair condition Tuesday after being pulled off the southbound Silver Star in Starke, Fla., on Sunday.

He had boarded the Capitol Limited in Chicago on Friday. Because flooding had closed some stations, he was bused with other passengers from Pittsburgh to Washington, D.C., where he got on the Silver Star. Greyhound Lines Inc. has been notified. In all, the two trains made 35 stops in 10 states.

"There's a very low chance that anyone would be affected," said Amtrak spokesman Rob Borella. He said the passenger's conclusive test results won't be available until later this week.

Tuberculosis is spread through the air and usually affects the lungs.

Amtrak gave the Centers for Disease Control and Prevention in Atlanta the names of passengers and crew who may have been exposed.

Six rail cars were pulled from service for cleaning, and air filters will be changed.

USA TODAY, 26 JANUARY, 1996

More viral outbreaks like Ebola feared

By Anita Manning
USA TODAY

Changes in ecology and human behavior are paving the way for rare viruses to emerge, virologists warned Tuesday.

Scientists at a meeting of the American Society for Microbiology in Washington, D.C., stressed the need to fund medical research and surveillance in preparation for outbreaks such as the Ebola virus epidemic that has killed more than 100 people in Zaire since mid-April.

Dr. C.J. Peters of the Centers for Disease Control and Prevention predicted his agency will spend about $1 million on the Ebola outbreak, and said he expects there will be "a couple hundred cases" in Zaire before it is over.

The disease, which causes fever and death from massive bleeding in up to 90% of cases, remains a mystery. "We don't understand the reservoir or history at all," Peters said.

Two suspected cases have been reported in Kinshasa, Zaire, a city of nearly 5 million. If confirmed, they would be the first to reach the capital, about 300 miles from Kikwit, where most of the cases have occurred.

In Rome, Father Don Arturo Bellini, a spokesman for the Little Sisters of the Poor, said a sixth nun has died of the disease in Kikwit and one more has symptoms of it. Annelvira Ossoli, 58, mother superior for her order's nuns in Africa, died after going to Kikwit to help care for her sisters, he said.

A medical surveillance team tracking cases has focused on a forest worker in Kikwit who died in late December 1994, and who may have been the first case in the epidemic.

Researchers Tuesday were heading for the forest region where the man worked, to trap animals and insects in a search for the source of the virus.

USA TODAY, 24 MAY, 1995

Vice President for Fast-Food Restaurant Quality Assurance

DR. DAVID THENO
FOODMAKER, INC.
(JACK-IN-THE-BOX
FAST-FOOD RESTAURANTS)
SAN DIEGO, CALIFORNIA

I am responsible for product quality and safety for a western and midwestern fast-food restaurant chain called Jack-in-the-Box. I'm also in charge of research and development as well as operational services.

We have very high health standards for our employees and products. Helping stop the spread of infectious disease in our local communities is a high priority for us. When there were reports of hepatitis near one of our restaurants, our investigators examined case studies of the children and adults infected. They found that children were spreading the disease at a local preschool.

As your team tries to find the cause of the disease in your community, carefully study the cases. Look for clues and patterns. Try to find the source of the infection. Is the disease coming from water, food, or person-to-person contact?

If you find a water-borne infection, tell people to boil their drinking and cooking water. They can also use bottled water.

If you suspect a food-borne disease, look for common exposure at a cafeteria, restaurant, or picnic. Possible diseases might include *E. coli* from undercooked ground beef, or salmo-

nella from poorly handled chicken.

If *E. coli* is the problem, make sure people understand that they should not eat rare or medium-rare hamburgers. Tell them to break every hamburger in half. If it is pink or red in the middle, they should send it back. Infections from undercooked meat are especially dangerous for children. Young children's abilities to fight infection are not as well developed.

If you suspect person-to-person transmission, you need to identify infected individuals as quickly as possible. Keep them away from other members of your community. We train our restaurant managers to be on the lookout for various symptoms of disease. They send employees home immediately if they see any sign of disease.

I grew up in an agricultural area. I worked with animals and was around veterinarians. We raised hunting dogs, horses, and

cattle in northern Illinois and southern Wisconsin. I was interested in the food industry at a young age.

As a graduate student, I taught several classes in food science to other graduate students. One course was parasitology—the study of parasites. Parasites are living things that live on or in another living organism. I went on to earn my doctorate in food science.

After several different jobs in the food industry, I started a consulting company. We provided quality technology for all kinds of food companies. One day, Foodmaker Incorporated, the company that owns Jack-in-the-Box restaurants, sought our help. There was an *E. coli* outbreak. *E. coli* bacteria live in everyone's intestines. Usually *E. coli* aren't harmful, but under certain conditions, they cause infection and become very dangerous.

I liked working with Foodmaker as a consultant, so I decided to work for them full time. I helped them develop and put into action an excellent program for assuring the quality of their food products.

If you are interested in a career in the food business, there are two ways to get there. One path is through the biological sciences. Start in high school with biology. Also take botany and microbiology if your school offers them. Horticulture, animal production, and animal agriculture are courses to take at the college level.

The other path to the food industry is engineering. There will be a lot of employment opportunities in equipment and process engineering. A machine is nothing more than a contraption that performs a task. Engineering teaches you how machines work.

In the food business, there are lots of jobs. Try a summer job or an internship. You could work in a grocery store or restaurant, harvesting agricultural products, or processing fruits and vegetables.

My knowledge of food safety makes me more careful about food handling at home. Here are the rules to follow to protect yourself from food-borne diseases such as salmonella and *E. coli*.

First, never defrost meat on a counter. Defrost it in a refrigerator, use a microwave, or place it under running water. Bacteria lie on the outside of most food products. When placed on a counter, the surface will quickly warm to near room temperature. Bacteria grow rapidly at room temperature.

When handling raw protein products such as fish and poul-

try, don't let their juices contaminate surfaces and other foods that will not be cooked. Bacteria can survive for several hours on your hands, counter tops, hand towels, and utensils. Wiping a counter top with a paper towel is not good enough. Use water and soap.

In our restaurants, we use simple and practical methods to protect people from diseases. We handle all protein products as if they contain potential disease-producing organisms.

Understanding the science of food handling can keep you healthy, and sometimes can save your life.

The Ebola outbreak was really scary. People were traveling to Kinshasa from Kikwit. We were afraid that they might bring Ebola to us. Then we would be bleeding all over.

My mom put some stuff in the water to purify it. When we went to the market to buy food, mom was careful about what she bought. We did not eat raw fruits or vegetables during that time.

We knew people in Kikwit. My dad worked with the church there. My dad's parents lived in Kikwit too. They didn't go out very much. Even in their neighborhoods, they never said "hi!" to each other. They stayed in their own houses, trying to kill the time by reading or listening to the news.

Even in Kinshasa, we worried a lot during the outbreak. I'm not worried now. I know that it's over now. I hope it won't come back again, and that they will find a cure for it.

MUHAWU LUMEYA
ZAIRIAN
KINSHASA, ZAIRE

Potent diseases develop and spread as the world shrinks

By Anita Manning
USA TODAY

New bugs are emerging and old ones are making a comeback, thanks to a combination of forces from genetic evolution to global climate change, say doctors and scientists who attended an American Medical Association briefing Tuesday.

The advent of antibiotics and improvements in public health systems helped to lull the medical community into a false sense of complacency, says Dr. George D. Lundberg, editor of the *Journal of the American Medical Association.*

"We humans were getting pretty cocky about our domination over other creatures," Lundberg says. "Then came genital herpes ... that was a wake-up call for the AIDS epidemic."

Today's *Journal,* along with 36 medical journals in 21 countries this month, devotes much of its editorial space to the subject of global microbial threats. The purpose, Lundberg says, is to "stimulate research, call worldwide attention to the issues and influence public policy."

One goal is to alert doctors to the dangers of overuse of antibiotics, a factor in the evolution of drug-resistant bacteria, Lundberg says.

One study in today's *Journal* looked at 419 adults admitted to hospitals in Columbus, Ohio, with strep pneumonia between January 1991 and April 1994. Dr. Joseph F. Plouffe of Ohio State University Medical Center and colleagues found the incidence of drug-resistant strains of the bacteria increased over the course of the study.

In 1991, only 4% of the pneumonia isolates wouldn't respond to penicillin, Plouffe says. By 1994, 14% of the strains were immune.

"Excessive antibiotic use appears to be the driving force behind the spread" of drug-resistant strep pneumonia, the authors write.

Another *Journal* report suggests

Fighting mutating microbes

Humans are in a race against evolving microbes, says molecular biologist Joshua Lederberg.

Lederberg, president emeritus of New York's Rockefeller University and author of a commentary in today's special issue of the *Journal of the American Medical Association,* says the challenge of emerging and re-emerging diseases is a matter of "microbial evolution versus our social intelligence — our wits."

While mankind has the advantage of "fabulous scientific knowledge," he says, the "sheer growth of human population ... its density, stratification, economic and social factors and international travel unprecedented in the human species" have created an environment in which a disease can emerge anywhere and spread rapidly around the world.

There is cause for concern, he says, but not alarm. "Many people feel helpless because it's not a matter the individual can influence. It's a matter of policy and politics. It has to be a public movement," he says.

"We've been nodding on the watch. We've been complacent. But there's something we can do about it."

Here's what he suggests:

▶ A concerted global and domestic system to monitor and diagnose disease outbreaks. Installation of sophisticated labs where needed.

▶ Monitoring and enforcement of safe water and food supplies.

▶ Public and professional education.

▶ Scientific research on vaccines, antibiotics, and causes and mechanisms of diseases.

▶ Cultivation of the fruits of such research, with public understanding of the regulations and incentives needed.

physicians need to be alert to the medical fallout that could result from global climate change.

This is "a relatively new issue in public health," says Dr. Jonathan A. Patz of the Johns Hopkins School of Public Health.

"Many infectious diseases are influenced by subtle shifts in climate," he says, citing heat-related deaths in cities and malnutrition from floods or crop failures in some regions.

"Malaria is likely to be the most sensitive infectious disease," he says. Its range is limited to tropical regions because the parasite that causes malaria doesn't survive in colder climates. But as global warming expands the region of warm weather, he says, it could bring malaria to "virgin populations that have no protective immunity."

Other diseases that could become more common as a result of global warming include dengue fever, African sleeping sickness, river blindness and St. Louis encephalitis. "Water-borne diseases such as cholera may also spread from rising sea-surface temperatures," he says.

However, he notes, "climate is not the only factor." Good sanitation, access to health care and clean water play a major role. And, while a warmer climate may expand the range of tropical illnesses, it also could reduce the incidence of such diseases as Rocky Mountain Spotted Fever, since the ticks that carry it might not survive warmer weather.

"My point is not that climate change necessarily has caused the re-emergence of these diseases," Patz says. "Rather in the context of anticipated changes in climate trends, our concern is that these diseases will spread into new areas or intensify in endemic regions."

Scientists have found evidence that climate change "is influenced by human activity and is expected to continue at an unprecedented rate over the next century," Patz says. "We need to consider prompt actions to avoid the impacts of such widespread environmental change."

USA TODAY, 17 JANUARY, 1996

Tetanus Anyone?

Purpose
To name bacteria using a dichotomous key.

Materials
• Reference materials

Background
You are the receptionist in a doctor's office. An eight-year-old girl just arrived with her mother. The girl had stepped on a rusty nail. As the mother gives you her insurance information, the little girl reads a poster titled "Common Bacteria in the World." A line under the title says, "Some of these bacteria are our friends . . . but some are our enemies! Can you tell which ones are which?" The poster has 11 drawings of bacteria on it.

The girl asks you to tell her the names of the bacteria. You cannot remember them all, but you know where the dichotomous key (a key dividing into two parts) is kept. You go to the file cabinet and take it out.

Procedure
Look at the bacteria shown above right and use the "Key to Bacteria Names" to identify them. Write their correct names on a piece of paper.

Conclusion
The little girl may have stepped on a rusty nail, but otherwise she is very bright. She has correctly identified all of the bacteria on the poster (with your help, of course). But she does not understand why she needs a tetanus booster shot. She's al-ready been stuck by a rusty nail, why does she have to be stuck by a hypodermic needle? She asks you what will happen to her if she does not have the tetanus shot and she *does* get the tetanus disease.

Prepare to explain the seriousness of tetanus to the little girl. Research the tetanus disease using sources inside this book and elsewhere. Write your findings in note form so you can explain the facts to other children too. Be sure to include where tetanus germs are found, how they enter the body, and how tetanus affects the body.

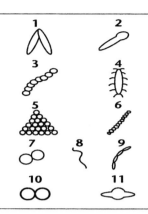

Bacteria Names:
Treponema pallidum (syphilis)
Diplococcus pneumoniae (pneumonia)
Streptococcus pyogenes (tonsillitis)
Streptococcus lactis (buttermilk)
Staphylococcus aureus (boils)
Bacillus anthracis (anthrax)
Bacillus lactis (sauerkraut)
Salmonella typhosa (typhoid fever)
Clostridium botulinum (botulism poisoning)
Clostridium tetani (tetanus)
Neisseria meningitidis (spinal meningitis)

Key to Bacteria Names
• If the general shape of the parts of the bacterium is **round**, go to **A**.
• If the general shape of the parts of the bacterium is **rod**, go to **B**.
• If the general shape of the parts of the bacterium is **spiral**, go to **C**.

A if in **pairs**, go to **a**; if in **chains**, go to **b**; if in **clumps**, go to **c**

a	without heavy cover	*Neisseria meningitidis*
	with heavy cover	*Diplococcus pneumoniae*
b	larger diameter	*Streptococcus pyogenes*
	smaller diameter	*Streptococcus lactis*
c		*Staphylococcus aureus*

B if in **chains**, go to **d**; if in **pairs**, go to **e**; if **single**, go to **f**

d		*Bacillus anthracis*
e		*Bacillus lactis*
f	with hairs (flagella)	*Salmonella typhosa*
	with middle bulge	*Clostridium botulinum*
	with bulge at one end	*Clostridium tetani*

C *Treponema pallidum*

In general, the word *bacillus* refers to rod-shaped bacteria, *coccus* refers to spherical, and *spirillus* refers to spiral-shaped.

Tetanus

Tetanus is a bacterial disease often called *lockjaw*. Tetanus germs form spores that can survive in the soil despite extreme conditions that would kill most other germs. Neither drought, nor heat, nor cold can kill the *Clostridium tetani* germs.

Tetanus enters the body through a wound in the skin. Any wound will do! It does not take a deep puncture for tetanus to start.

When tetanus spores become activated by the decomposing tissues at the site of a wound, the growing germs release a deadly toxin. Their poison moves rapidly, using the nerves as a pathway.

Once in the spinal cord, the *tetanus toxin* causes muscles throughout the body to contract in uncontrolled spasms. A gruesome smile often locks onto the faces of its victims. One in four tetanus victims die a very painful death.

There are two methods for fighting back against tetanus. You can have long-term, active immunization by having an injection of *tetanus toxoid*, or you can receive an injection of tetanus antitoxin after an injury. Tetanus toxoid is a deactivated form of the toxin that causes our bodies to produce a natural antitoxin. This method works well to protect us, especially if we receive a booster every ten years.

The tetanus antitoxin is less effective against tetanus. The antibodies used to provide this passive immunity are produced in horses that are especially sensitive to the tetanus toxin. Passive immunization only works if it is injected a day or two after injury—the quicker the better.

Active Versus Passive Immunity

If you have already had a good case of the viral disease chicken pox, you are immune to it. That means you will not get chicken pox again. There are two main ways that your body becomes immune to disease—active immunity and passive immunity.

Active immunity happens when a disease germ or other foreign substance actually invades your body. White blood cells called *lymphocytes* react by making antibodies to destroy the invader. Active immunity also results when you are vaccinated with a deactivated germ.

In both examples, your body has to recognize an invader and make antibodies against it. Also, active immunity leaves your body ready to recognize future invasions by the same germ and to respond so quickly that you never again get as sick from it.

Passive immunity is different. In passive immunity, antibodies are taken from another source and injected into you. Passive immunity lasts only a short time. It actually tricks your body into not producing antibodies.

Although passive immunity does not provide lasting protection, doctors can use it if you have already contracted a serious infection and would likely die without treatment.

Rabies immunity is an example of the two types of immunity. Rabies is a fatal viral disease of the brain of mammals. It is usually transmitted when a diseased animal bites a healthy one. Dogs and cats are vaccinated against rabies. This gives them an active immunity.

People are rarely vaccinated against rabies, but if a rabid animal bites you, a doctor can inject you with a serum containing rabies antibodies. This gives you a temporary—passive—immunity.

What's In It for You?

Purpose

To use microscopes to examine samples of water and food for the presence of microorganisms.

Materials

For each group:
- Notebook or pad
- Compound microscope
- Microscope slide
- Cover slip
- Lens paper
- Methylene blue stain
- Paper towels
- Labeled water samples (from a lake, a water fountain, and a restaurant)
- Food samples from two community restaurants
- Toothpicks
- Reference materials

Background

Some human diseases are caused by contaminated water and food. Could the disease hitting your community be coming from those sources? The city council suggests you sample water and food in the community.

Create a chart that includes the following items:
- a list of the names of samples examined
- a description of the organisms found
- identification of the kind(s) of organisms found
- the organisms' relative numbers (use words such as *few*, *some*, and *many*)

Do your best work! After you finish, send your data chart to a scientist at the Centers for Disease Control (your teacher).

Procedure

1. Read all instructions. With your team, brainstorm the things you need to know and do to complete this activity.
2. Use the materials provided to examine each water and food sample under high magnification. *Hint:* If you put a piece of thread from a cotton ball in the wet mount, it will make it easier to focus the microscope.
3. Draw diagrams of organisms that you find in each sample.
4. Try to identify the organisms you find by name. Use reference materials.
5. Complete your chart with the information requested.

Conclusion

Before you prepare a final copy of your data chart, discuss your results with students from some of the other teams that have been examining the same samples. How do your observations compare to theirs? Using all information available to you, write a paragraph summarizing your conclusions. Is the disease coming from the food or water?

Before you write, think about the following questions (discuss these questions if you need to):

1. If bacteria are present in a water or food sample, does that mean a disease is present? Explain.
2. Why can't viruses be seen with the microscope you used?
3. What other disease agents besides bacteria and viruses might be found in water or food?
4. How does your community make sure its water is safe?
5. How does the food industry make sure its products do not carry diseases?
6. What can you do to protect your family members from getting sick from water or food contamination?

Ebola is apparently contained

By Anita Manning
USA TODAY

No new cases have been reported since May 25 in the outbreak of Ebola virus in Zaire, says Bob Howard of the Centers for Disease Control and Prevention. "It appears we have our arms around" the epidemic, which has killed 173 of 220 known victims, he says.

The World Health Organization, coordinating international medical relief, said new cases may occur in people still in the incubation period, but "transmission seems now to be completely halted."

The virus, for which there is no treatment or vaccine,

causes vomiting, diarrhea and massive bleeding. It has killed about 75% of victims in this outbreak, say WHO officials.

Efforts now are focused on beefing up health services in the afflicted region near Kikwit, east of Zaire's capital, Kinshasa, and on trying to find the virus's hiding place in nature.

An "ecology crew" of about 11 people, including two Somali health educators, two U.S. Army doctors and a group of CDC scientists, is converging on Kikwit, says Howard, to "begin the process to determine what the host of this virus is." They will work with veterinarians in Zaire to capture and examine bats, rats and other animals in the Kikwit region.

USA TODAY, 7 JUNE, 1995

Making a Wet Mount

Place a drop of the specimen you wish to examine in the center of a clean, dry microscope slide. If the specimen is small and dry, add a drop of water or liquid stain to it. Place a cover slip over the specimen and observe it under the microscope. Be sure to begin on the lowest power.

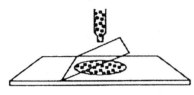

There is a right way and a wrong way to use the highest power of your microscope. The wrong way is the way most people think of first—put the slide on the stage of the microscope, move the high-power objective into place, and look through the eyepiece. But, finding anything this way is almost impossible.

The first thing you should do is examine the specimen using the lowest power your microscope has. Focus the scope and explore the slide. Move anything you wish to examine in more detail to the center of the field of light. Now revolve the nosepiece of your microscope until the next higher power snaps into place. With some microscopes, the specimen will still be in focus. In others, you need to use the fine adjustment. A few microscopes might even require complete refocusing at this point.

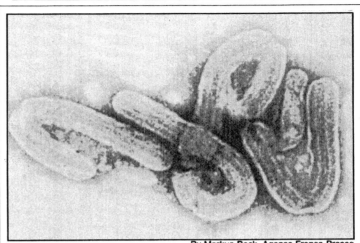

By Markus Beck, Agence France-Presse

EBOLA: The Marburg virus strain appeared in Germany in 1967 at a lab of African monkeys and killed about 25% of those infected.

How the virus spreads and where it thrives

World Health Organization experts in Zaire said Wednesday the number of Ebola cases has jumped to 101; 77 have died. More cases are expected to be announced by Friday as health workers complete house-to-house checks.

Officials continue to assure people that the virus is not airborne and can only be spread through contact with blood and other body fluids. Contact with people who are infected but have no symptoms is not likely to cause transmission of the virus, experts say.

"The major means of transmission appears to be close and unprotected patient contact or preparation of the dead for burial," says a WHO statement.

The Centers for Disease Control and Prevention has set up a hot line that gives information on the virus, 800-900-0681.

Virus facts:

▶ Ebola Zaire is the deadliest member of a family of viruses called filoviruses. In previous outbreaks, it killed 90% of those infected. Under an electron microscope, filoviruses look like threads. Other forms are Ebola Sudan, which kills about 50% of its victims, and Marburg virus, which appeared in the German city of Marburg in 1967 at a lab full of African monkeys. It killed about 25% of those it infected.

▶ Symptoms, which begin four to 16 days after infection, include fever, chills, headaches, muscle aches and appetite loss. As it progresses, the virus causes vomiting, diarrhea, abdominal pain, sore throat and chest pain. Blood fails to clot, bleeding is massive.

▶ Diagnosis is made by detection of Ebola antibodies or isolation of the virus in body fluids.

▶ Ebola was discovered in 1976 and named for the Ebola River in Zaire, where it was first detected. Another outbreak occurred in 1976 in western Sudan. In those outbreaks, 550 cases were reported, 340 people died. A third outbreak in Sudan in 1979 caused 34 cases and 22 deaths.

▶ The source of Ebola is unknown.

USA TODAY, 18 MAY, 1995

Lessons Learned

International teams of doctors and disease investigators responded to the Ebola outbreak in Kikwit. They made their way to the hot zone to offer assistance, but primitive conditions in Kikwit meant delays in containing the virus.

Medicines and supplies were nearly nonexistent. Hundreds of thousands of dollars worth of disposable protective clothing, blood plasma, and body bags had to be shipped in. Plastic hospital gowns and sterile needles were airlifted to the site.

Poor transportation and communications within the country frustrated the teams of specialists. There were few telephones and no radio station. Members of medical squads could not coordinate with each other. National health authorities in Zaire were difficult to reach. Lack of money and personnel also delayed the reaction to the fast-spreading Ebola.

The 1995 Ebola outbreak has sparked action. There is now support for setting up a global network to track infectious diseases. This network would use the Internet and World-Wide Web. Outbreaks can be detected, assessed, and responded to quickly. Researchers would quickly report news of outbreaks to field stations around the globe. A world-wide, rapid-alert system would deploy response teams and supplies to hot zones.

This kind of global effort requires money from developed countries around the world. Such organizations as the World Health Organization (WHO) in Geneva, Switzerland, and the U.S. Agency for International Development (USAID) could help organize and fund a disease surveillance network.

Better training for health authorities in poor nations is a critical factor in disease control and prevention. Training could minimize the threat of emerging diseases by speeding up detection and containment of outbreaks.

Nobody can predict just how fatal the next virus

STUDENT VOICES

I heard about the Ebola outbreak on CNN. At first, I was not scared. Then my dad explained it to me, and I was really scared.

During the outbreak, we bought imported fruits and vegetables. We stayed away from restaurants, too. We were more careful about where we went and who we spoke to.

This was the first disease I experienced outside of my country. I was really surprised at how everybody got so scared. People were saying that everybody was going to get it and that we were all going to die.

I don't like blood. I don't want it coming out of every single place on me. We're not worried now though.

NAFISA TEJANI
CANADIAN
KINSHASA, ZAIRE

or bacterium will be or when and where it will appear. Infectious microbes know no borders. A mutation of the Ebola virus could be more deadly than the original. The spread of a killer virus from one country to another is just a plane ride away.

Why are infectious diseases such as Ebola emerging? The causes are not understood. Some scientists suggest a link to global climate change. Other experts believe environmental disturbances such as deforestation of tropical rain forests could be stirring up infectious organisms.

More and more, species that might carry a virus, bacterium, or other disease germ come into contact with humans. As more people enter new ecological habitats, particularly in Africa, plowing soil and clearing forest, many new diseases may emerge.

Ebola infects monkeys, but infected monkeys die too fast to be the natural sanctuary of the virus. Mammals, insects, reptiles, birds, even plants have been considered possible hosts of the virus. So far, the true reservoir of Ebola has not been detected. Few clues exist.

People who survived contact with Ebola in the Kikwit outbreak might provide clues. Most who endured the virus received transfusions of blood. The blood came from survivors of previous Ebola outbreaks. The blood contained *antibodies*—particles that recognize and kill a specific invading germ. Why these survivors did not die from infection in the first place remains a puzzle.

Meanwhile, the terror called Ebola has gone back into hiding. Without warning, its destructive nature might surface again.

Science knows little about mad cow disease

By Anita Manning
USA TODAY

Recent visitors to Great Britain are concerned about reports last week by British health officials that there may be a link between mad cow disease and 10 cases of Creutzfeldt-Jakob disease, or CJD.

Mad cow disease, formally known as bovine spongiform encephalopathy, makes infected animals clumsy and nervous. CJD is a similar disorder in humans that may not occur until years after infection.

There is no mad cow disease in the USA, health officials say, but Britain is the No. 1 overseas destination for U.S. travelers. Many of the millions of U.S. visitors each year consume beef while there. Could they be at risk for CJD?

Dr. Larry Schonberger of the Centers for Disease Control and Prevention, Atlanta, spoke to USA TODAY about it:

Q. What does it do to people and how is it treated?

A. It destroys the nerves, causing confusion and rapidly progressive dementia. It is 100% fatal. Patients die in about seven months.

Q. Is it a virus?

A. No one has the absolute, definite answer. The prevailing hypothesis is that the agent is a protein, an abnormal form of what is usually a normal component of cell surface.

Q. Is it a new disease?

A. BSE was identified by the British in 1986. Some people hypothesize it was always there, in a very low frequency, and nobody recognized it.

Q. England changed the way cattle are raised to protect its food supply, true?

A. The full protective measures they instituted were completed around 1989.

Q. What is the incubation period?

A. It depends on the route of infection. In the one example where we have good information, the injection of people with human growth hormone (from the pituitary gland of an infected corpse), the incubation period is about 20 years. But it can be shorter or longer.

Q. How long would it be when it's in food?

A. That route of transmission hasn't been (recognized) before, so that's new. It's not clear (the 10 British cases) in fact got the disease from cattle, or from eating beef. An advisory group reported that based on a lack of a credible alternative explanation. It is considered the best explanation at this time.

Q. Is it possible there are more cases about to emerge after a long incubation?

A. That is what the British committee has suggested, that this will not be the end of it.

Q. Is there a test to tell if someone is carrying CJD?

A. No.

Q. Can it be passed from person to person?

A. No. This is not a disease that jumps out at you. You can have close relations with someone sick with this disease and not be at risk. With those 10 cases, they're saying the pattern is different. There may be something brewing here.

Q. If someone ate roast beef or steak-and-kidney pie in England in 1988, should he or she be concerned?

A. If I were them, I'd be concerned with what's going on. I'd want to follow it, to see if the hypothesis is true (that it came from eating beef), and to see what the extent of the risk is.

▶ **Mad cow disease, 8A**

USA TODAY, 27 MARCH, 1996

Quarantine

Some diseases are very contagious. They spread easily from person to person. Contagious diseases can spread by direct contact, through the air, in water, or in food.

Sometimes the only way to stop the spread of a disease is with a quarantine. *Quarantine* is the act of keeping healthy people from coming in contact with sick people. Quarantines are also used to stop the spread of diseases from plant to plant, from animal to animal, and from animal to human.

If you are considering a quarantine for your community, you must answer important questions. What is causing the disease you are trying to contain? How is the disease transmitted? How long does it take symptoms to appear after a person is infected? How long does a person remain infectious after symptoms appear?

During the Middle Ages (from about the sixth to the sixteenth centuries) in Europe, bubonic plague killed millions of people over many years. In those days, no one knew that germs caused disease. Doctors did not know how to prevent that terrible disease from spreading.

In the fourteenth century, the Italian city of Venice started quarantining sailing ships arriving at port. They thought a 40-day quarantine would help control the plague. The quarantine meant crew members could not leave their ships. That way,

the sailors would not carry the disease into the city.

It did not work. Infected fleas living on rats aboard the ships were the real carriers of the plague. The rats easily scurried off the ships to spread the plague through the city.

A similar problem struck nineteenth century European cities. People infected with cholera were quarantined. Cholera is a disease caused by bacteria and is spread in water. A century ago, people did not have sewage treatment. They often had contaminated water supplies. It was impossible to completely isolate infected people from the public water supply.

Today, most countries have water purification and sewage treatment. Air-quality control, refrigeration, food processing,

and pest control are also common. Even jumbo jets filter air through the same high-efficiency air filters used in laboratories studying the most dangerous germs. These technological developments make it easier to control the spread of germs.

What about extremely contagious diseases, such as the Ebola virus? Researchers wear protective outfits that look like space suits to shield themselves from contamination. Protective clothing can keep out germs spread by air, water, or physical contact.

Technological advances have, however, made quarantines harder to enforce. World travel has become more popular. It is very hard to keep contagious diseases from spreading around the globe.

Virus same strain as in '76

By Leslie Miller
USA TODAY

The strain of Ebola virus behind the current outbreak in Zaire is the same one that caused previous epidemics in the 1970s, the World Health Organization confirmed Sunday.

That may be a positive sign: "It doesn't appear to have mutated into something new," said WHO spokesman Christopher Powell.

But he said little is known about the virus, discovered in 1976: "Nobody's managed to find where the reservoir is."

Officials also hope to isolate the virus' carrier, possibly monkeys, bats or insects, he said. "It's hard to find because it is such a rare virus."

WHO's team in Kikwit, Zaire, Sunday reported three new cases and two deaths.

There is no treatment or vaccine, but good hygiene and standard protective measures can prevent its spread.

The government of Sudan is skeptical: It will quarantine all travelers from Zaire.

Officials say such measures are extreme. The virus has a short incubation and victims are generally too ill to travel.

WHO said there is no confirmation of new cases outside of Kikwit, but teams today will fan out to see if reports of the virus in four towns are true.

If confirmed, the new cases would be 125 miles east of Kinshasa, more than halfway to the capital.

USA TODAY, 15 MAY, 1995

School Principal

MRS. BETTY GREER
HARTIGAN SCHOOL
CHICAGO, ILLINOIS

Before becoming a principal, I was a teacher. I wanted to become a teacher because I was inspired and encouraged by outstanding teachers I had. Most of these were my high school teachers who took special interest in their students.

My home economics teacher, for example, gave me a high sense of self-esteem. She encouraged me. Because she and others were so outstanding, I decided to become an educator too.

During my teaching career, two principals were my mentors. They convinced me that if I wanted to influence the lives of more students than just the 30 in my own classroom, I should become a principal. Having strong ties to the community and to parents also led me to become a principal.

If becoming a principal interests you, do your best in all your classes at school. At the college level, in addition to general requirements for your degree, education courses inform you about teaching methods and school administration.

I earned a bachelor's degree in education and a master's degree in reading. After teaching for a few years, I went back to school to earn my degree in administration and supervision.

It is important that principals have a good understanding of curriculum development. They also need courses in communication. Good communication skills help you work better with parents, children, teachers, and others in the community. Of course, knowing how to use computers is very important also.

As a principal, I observe classes and interact with children every day. If children disobey school rules, my job is to counsel them. I give them an opportunity to explain their perspective of what happened.

Helping students try to correct their behavior is an important part of being a principal. I use positive support and have them look ahead. How might they handle the situation differently if it occurred again? There are times when we have to suspend students. There are firm rules in our school.

Our student body's health is very important to us. The Chicago Public Schools require students to have a physical examination in kindergarten, first, third, fifth, and eighth grades. Children must have all their vaccinations before they come to school. This helps protect them and other students against diseases.

We still deal with a lot of colds and flus. We always call parents when kids have the flu or are not feeling well.

Our school is currently participating in an asthma study with Loyola University. In this program, a pediatrician and nurse test the children. Researchers study and track the children to understand factors that contribute to asthma. They check to see if the number of people with the illness is increasing. These children are also taught about their illness and how to protect themselves.

As a principal, I also deal with gym and athletic injuries. When the nurse is not available, the physical education teacher can administer first aid and CPR. When a child is injured, we contact the parents and the Chicago Police Department. The police contact the Chicago Fire Department to send a medic.

I know of cases of tuberculosis (TB) in our community, but we have not had TB or other serious contagious diseases in our school. Doctors tested the children in the family that had tuberculosis. We made sure they didn't have the disease.

The school has simple procedures for handling an outbreak of an infectious disease. We identify all students with the illness and isolate them. Children with a disease such as TB can continue to go to school under one condition: A doctor must tell us the children are receiving medication and cannot harm other children. We monitor those children carefully.

With some diseases, the health department says the children must stay at home to stop the spread of the disease. For example, when children have pink eye, a very contagious eye disease, we immediately send them to the nurse. The nurse bans them from school until they are well. If a child is excluded from school, he or she must bring a doctor's certificate to be readmitted.

One year we had a second grader who had leukemia—a cancer of the bone marrow. Leukemia is not a contagious disease, but she had treatments that caused her to lose her hair. That was frightening to some of the children. We let her wear a cap her teachers decorated with bows. The other children learned about her disease and were very kind to her.

Principals are responsible for creating a safe and healthy environment in which all children can learn. That means we must take care of both the mental and physical needs of children and staff in our schools.

Quarantine slapped on Zaire city

By Jack Kelley
USA TODAY

Zaire closed schools, canceled flights and ordered people off the streets in the city of Kikwit Thursday as the mysterious Ebola virus continued its deadly course.

Nearly 100 people have been killed in Kikwit, 370 miles east of the capital of Kinshasa, by the virus or bloody diarrhea related to the viral illness. Officials have declared the city a disaster zone and slapped a quarantine on it.

Kinshasa's governor closed the capital to anyone traveling from the infected area, leaving thousands of villagers stranded.

"If the disease penetrates to Kinshasa, that will be a catastrophe," said governor Bernadin Mungul Diaka.

Also, a U.S. Air Force C-141 cargo

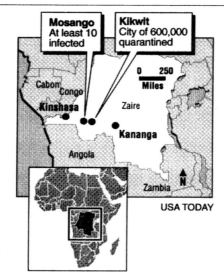

Mosango
At least 10 infected

Kikwit
City of 600,000 quarantined

0   250
Miles

Gabon
Congo
Kinshasa
Zaire
Kananga
Angola
Zambia
N

USA TODAY

plane loaded with body bags, plasma and protective clothing left for Zaire as teams from the Atlanta-based Centers for Disease Control and Prevention arrived to analyze the virus.

Meanwhile, a third Italian nun who worked at the Kikwit hospital, 48-year-old Danielangelina Sorti, died of Ebola.

Two other members of the Little Sisters of the Poor order are in serious but stable condition. Twelve other nuns are still working there, said spokeswoman Sister Mauricia.

"We will continue our work, despite the risks. We cannot abandon them now," Sister Mauricia said, struggling to hold back tears.

Officials are also investigating a second outbreak of the virus in a 350-bed hospital in the Zairian village of Musango, 60 miles from Kikwit, after a nurse died.

"We don't know where the disease came from and we're not sure where it has spread," says Veerle Eygenraam of the aid group Doctors Without Borders.

Like the AIDS virus, Ebola is transmitted through body fluids and secretions, not casual contact. It causes extreme fever and severe hemorrhaging within days. Ninety percent of those affected die. There is no known treatment or vaccine.

It's "one of the deadliest viruses we know," says Dr. Ralph Henderson, assistant director of the Geneva-based World Health Organization.

Still, doctors are urging people to stay calm.

"It is unlikely that this outbreak will have implications for Zaire as a whole or for international travel," Henderson says.

USA TODAY, 10 MAY, 1995

Famous Disease Fighters

Edward Jenner (1749–1823) was a British doctor who discovered the vaccine against smallpox. His work forms the basis for today's science of immunology. In Jenner's time, smallpox was a major cause of death. Jenner noticed that anyone who had cowpox, a mild relative of smallpox, usually did not get smallpox. In May of 1796, Jenner injected a boy with the fluid from a blister on a milkmaid who had cowpox. Of course the boy came down with cowpox. Six weeks later, after the boy recovered from cowpox, Jenner inoculated him with blister fluid from a person sick with smallpox. The boy remained healthy. At first people did not want to believe Jenner's discovery worked. Within a few years, though, the procedure was accepted. Death from smallpox became rare, and smallpox vaccinations have been discontinued in this country.

Ignaz Philipp Semmelweis (1818–1865) was a Hungarian obstetrician. In the 1840s, he discovered that hand washing prevented infections in the maternity hospital where he worked. Semmelweis noticed that childbed fever killed 30 percent of women who gave birth in clinics, while women who gave birth at home rarely died of the fever. Clinics at the time were very dirty places. Doctors' lab coats were typically stained with blood from many patients. Doctors used surgical instruments again and again with only a quick rinse between patients. By experimenting with antiseptic practices, Semmelweis reduced the death rate from childbed fever to less than 1 percent. His discovery of the importance of cleanliness is basic to preventing the spread of infection in hospitals and homes throughout the world today.

Louis Pasteur (1822–1895) was a French chemist and biologist. He is known as the father of the science of microbiology, which is the study of microscopic life. We remember him especially for his development of the germ theory of disease. Pasteur believed microscopic germs attacked the body from the outside. Many scientists disagreed and believed germs were spontaneously produced in substances themselves. People of his day found the idea of tiny organisms killing larger ones ridiculous. Pasteur's studies proved he was right. Over the course of his life, he showed that germs caused many different diseases.

Sir Alexander Fleming (1881–1955) was a British bacteriologist. We remember him especially for his discovery of penicillin in 1928. The discovery was accidental. When Fleming was doing research on influenza, he noticed mold growing on one of his culture plates. He almost threw the plate away because the mold had destroyed the bacteria growing on it. Then he stopped himself—perhaps the mold was making a chemical that could destroy bacteria in the body too. That chemical, penicillin, has helped millions of people recover from all sorts of infections. Fleming's discovery earned him the 1945 Nobel Prize in physiology and medicine.

Jonas Salk (1914–1995) was an American doctor and medical researcher. His work on a vaccine against influenza led him to develop an injected vaccine against polio in 1952. In the mid-1950s, health workers distributed the vaccine nationwide. The vaccine greatly reduced the number of people who died or became paralyzed by polio. Along with the oral vaccine against polio developed by Dr. Albert Sabin a few years later, Salk's discovery brought polio under control.

An Ounce of Cure

Purpose

To investigate the effects of different medicines on pathogens.

Materials

For the team:
- Petri dish with nutrient agar
- Spray bottle labeled "Pathogens"
- 3 small circles of filter paper soaked in medicines
- Glass-marking pencil or crayon
- Cellophane tape
- Notebook paper
- At least 2 sheets of blank paper
- At least 1 sheet of grid paper

Background

Several physicians in your neighborhood have failed in their attempts to cure the rapidly spreading disease. Doctors usually cure bacterial diseases with traditional antibiotic therapy. This disease is resistant to everything the doctors have tried so far. What can be done to help these patients and prevent the spread of their disease?

A scientist in a research laboratory has successfully isolated disease-causing bacteria from the blood of some patients. The blood was taken from people who were treated but did not get well. To help the laboratory, your task team must quickly determine the effectiveness of different medicines on these bacteria. Time is running out!

Procedure

Caution: Be sure not to touch your face with your hands during this lab! Chemicals used in this lab can be harmful if they come in contact with your eyes or mouth!

1. Your supervisor (teacher) will give you a sterile petri dish with nutrient agar. Keep the petri dish closed except when you are adding something. Always close it quickly. Label your dish with your team name, using a glass-marking pencil or crayon.
2. Use the glass marker to draw four equal sections on the petri dish without touching the nutrient agar. Make a map of the dish on a sheet of notebook paper.
3. As a team, select three medicines to test with the disease-causing organism. The medicines are on circles of filter paper. Use tweezers to place the three circles you chose in three different marked sections of your petri dish. These medicines have been effective against the disease in the past. The fourth section is a control—do not add medicine there.
4. On your map, label which quadrant of the dish is the control. Label the other three quadrants with the code names of the medicines that you are testing.
5. Test the spray bottle by pointing it into a sink and squeezing its handle until you see a fine mist. Allow the mist to settle in the sink, then rinse the sink.
6. Place the petri dish in a sink, then open it. Simulate a sneeze or cough by holding the spray bottle at the top of the sink and pointing it toward the petri dish. Spray *once*. Spray quickly and firmly. This will evenly distribute the mist over the surface of the nutrient agar. Allow the mist to settle for about 10 seconds, then close the petri dish.
7. Tape the cover to the petri dish. Put the dish upside down in a warm, dark place.
8. With your team, discuss what might happen inside the petri dish. Think about how you will check the effectiveness of the three medicines.

Conclusion

The purpose of your research was to find the best treatment available to cure the disease spreading throughout your community. Prepare an illustrated report of your findings. The report will be submitted to the health department.

Describe the effectiveness of each of the medicines tested. Be sure to report on all of the medicines tested by your class. Make a graph to illustrate and summarize your findings.

In a paragraph, discuss your recommendation for the medicine to use against the disease. Be sure to explain why the usual antibiotics are not effective against this pathogen. (You will need to do research to find this out.)

Noninfectious Diseases

Noninfectious diseases can be caused by environmental conditions, lack of good nutrition, birth or genetic defects, or physical stress. Sometimes a disease can cause a weakness that promotes another disease. Some types of diseases and a few examples are listed below. A disease can appear under more than one heading.

Chronic Degenerative Diseases

Some diseases start out unnoticed in the body, affecting only a few cells at first. Gradually these diseases progress. The tissues or muscles begin to degenerate, becoming less healthy. Sometimes the degeneration ends in death.

Cancer is a degenerative disease that can occur anywhere in the body. It causes cells in the body to divide and multiply abnormally. Eventually cancer cells destroy other cells.

Cardiovascular disease affects the heart and circulatory system, including the lungs, veins, and arteries. Nutrients and oxygen carried in the blood cannot reach the body's cells. The blood cannot remove the cells' waste products.

Arthritis inflames the joints. It is most common in the hands, knees, and hips and can be very painful. Arthritis can also be a symptom of other diseases.

Osteoporosis weakens the inside of the bones, making bones brittle. It is a health concern for many women and some men as they grow older and lose calcium. Increasing calcium intake and exercise can slow its progress.

Alzheimer's disease affects the brain and can make its middle-aged or older victims forgetful. Alzheimer's can lead to early death.

Amyotrophic lateral sclerosis (ALS) is often called *Lou Gehrig's disease* after the famous baseball player who died from this illness. It attacks the spinal cord and makes the muscles weak. Finally, the muscles waste away.

Multiple sclerosis (MS) affects the nervous system. It damages the outside casing of nerves in the brain and spinal cord. People with MS have difficulty walking and talking.

Autoimmune diseases occur when the body's immune system treats normal parts of the body like invaders. It makes antibodies to fight against these "invaders." What makes the body turn against parts of itself? Some scientists think viruses might play a role. In many autoimmune diseases, though, scientists just do not know yet.

Rheumatic fever is a delayed complication from a coldlike illness. Rheumatic fever affects the heart muscle and the membrane around the heart. Sometimes the heart never fully recovers.

Anemia occurs when blood does not have enough hemoglobin. Hemoglobin carries oxygen to your cells. In one kind of anemia, the body destroys its own red blood cells.

Allergies

Allergies are diseases in which the victim's immune system overreacts to particles of dust, dander, or pollen in the environment and produces the sneezing, stuffy nose, and watery eyes normally associated with the common cold. Food and airborne allergens can also produce skin rashes called *hives*.

Poison oak and *poison ivy* are allergic diseases caused by contact with the resin from these plants. An allergic person who has been in contact with the resin once will be sensitive to it in later contacts. Sufferers of poison oak or ivy get blisters with intense itching. Scratching makes the rash spread.

Hormonal Diseases

Hormones are the body's chemical messengers. The endocrine glands produce them. The bloodstream carries them to certain organs or body tissues. There they affect body processes such as growth, metabolism, and reproduction. Too much or not enough of a hormone upsets the normal balance in the body. Sometimes life cannot continue without the appropriate hormone balance. Often, however, these imbalances can be treated with synthetic hormones.

Diabetes results from a lack of the hormone insulin. Insulin is necessary to turn the carbohydrates you eat into energy. Diabetics must control their diets. Some diabetics take insulin injections.

Thyroid-related diseases come from too much or not enough thyroid hormone. A lack of thyroid hormone makes you feel tired and lifeless. Thyroid overactivity can lead to anxiety, increased heart rate, weight loss, and increased appetite.

Gigantism and *dwarfism* are caused by too much or too little of the growth hormone somatotropin. This hormone is stored in the pituitary gland and makes the long bones in the arms and legs grow.

Deficiency Diseases

Everyone needs vitamins and minerals in very small amounts for healthy growth and development. The body cannot make most of them. You have to get them from your diet. A lack of a vitamin or mineral can lead to big problems.

Scurvy is caused by a lack of vitamin C. Fruits and vegetables contain this vitamin. It is especially abundant in citrus fruits. The first sign of scurvy is bleeding gums. People can die from lack of vitamin C.

Beriberi results from a lack of vitamin B1 or thiamine. The disease leads to a degeneration of the nerves and eventually heart failure.

Rickets occurs when children do not get enough vitamin D. Bones do not harden properly and easily bend out of shape. Bowed legs and bloated stomachs are common characteristics of rickets.

Anemia is sometimes caused by lack of the mineral iron. Iron is needed to produce hemoglobin, which carries oxygen in the blood. Anemic people experience severe fatigue and get sick easily.

Goiter is an enlargement of the thyroid gland. The disease can be caused by a lack of the mineral iodine in the diet.

Many people in the United States take vitamin and mineral supplements in concentrated pill form. However, there is no evidence that taking pills is necessary for someone who eats a diet rich in fruits and vegetables.

Congenital Conditions

Congenital disorders are abnormalities that occur while a baby is developing in its mother's womb. Many develop during the first eight weeks of gestation and are present at birth. They can be caused by chemicals (drugs), radiation, or infectious diseases. Another cause of birth defects is a genetic defect in the fetus. Sometimes the problem is a single gene; sometimes it is an abnormality in the chromosome.

A *blue baby* is an infant born with a heart defect that permits unoxygenated blood to mix with oxygen-rich blood. The child's skin is a bluish color because blood with less oxygen is being pumped throughout its body. The blood itself is not blue. Blood without oxygen is brownish-maroon that appears bluish when viewed through layers of skin. Surgery can sometimes correct the problem. Unoxygenated blood turns red as it picks up oxygen in the lungs.

Down's syndrome results from having an extra number 21 chromosome. Children born with this disorder have mental retardation and characteristic physical abnormalities.

Hereditary Diseases

Hereditary diseases are those passed on from parent to child in the genes. A gene is the basic unit of genetic material. Genes determine everything about you, such as your eye and hair color, your body shape, and whether you have certain diseases or disorders. Many hereditary diseases are very rare. Some, described below, are more common.

Sickle-cell anemia is a hereditary blood disease that mostly affects people of African descent. People with this illness have a mutation in the gene responsible for making hemoglobin in red blood cells. The defective hemoglobin changes the red cells' shape so they cannot easily move through the smallest blood vessels, called *capillaries*. The body does not get enough oxygen. This results in pain and weakness.

Hemophilia slows blood clotting. Bleeding after an injury might go on for hours. Today, in-

Normal red cells   **Sickle cells**

home treatment makes hemophilia easier to manage. Hemophilia affects only the males in a family, but the genetic trait is carried by women and passed on to their sons.

Muscular dystrophy progressively weakens and wastes away certain muscles. It is usually discovered before the age of four. Muscular dystrophy attacks males almost exclusively, but the gene that causes it can be passed on by women.

Environmental Diseases

Environmental diseases include radiation sickness, toxin-related food poisoning, and diseases carried in water and air.

Immunity

Immunity means freedom from harassment. The human immune system works to defend the body from harassment by invaders.

Your senses usually warn you about potential dangers, but sometimes the threats are too small. Microscopic threats often cannot be seen, heard, smelled, touched, or tasted. Your immune system protects you even against the invisible—it is a personal security system.

Bacteria, viruses, fungi, protozoa, and other microscopic organisms are around all the time. They are in the air, in water, in your food, and on your skin. Humans live in a jungle of potential attackers. These attackers can make you sick if they find an open door into your body.

The immune system protects your body against all kinds of germs. It also fights off toxic materials (poisons) as well as irritants that can cause allergic reactions (allergens).

You are probably well most of the time, but sometimes the invaders get past your body's outermost defenses and make you sick. Your skin is the first barrier. If your skin is broken, germs can invade your body and cause infection. When a cut is attacked by bacteria, the infected spot gets red, hot, and swollen. This inflammation occurs because blood flow increases to the area, bringing with it a variety of immune-system weapons.

The mouth, nose, and other openings also let germs deep into the body. However, the linings of these openings provide a barrier to invasion.

Mucous and saliva, secreted by special cells in these linings, trap and flush out most invaders. Mucous and saliva are also parts of your first-line of defense. The germs you swallow are usually destroyed by stomach acid. Surviving germs pass into the intestines, where they can fall victim to the movement of waste material through the intestines. Feces carry germs out of the body.

Your body also contains friendly bacteria called *E. coli*. *E. coli* live on the undigested food in your large intestine. In return for a warm moist home, *E. coli* produce vitamin K—essential for blood clotting—and some of the B vitamins too.

The immune system has cells that attack bad cells directly. White blood cells called *phagocytes* do this work. Like security guards, phagocytes wander around the body looking for unwelcome visitors. Unlike security guards, when the phagocytes find an unwelcome visitor, they eat it.

Other white blood cells called *lymphocytes* make antibodies to attack the invading cells. One type of antibody kills invaders by making holes in their cell surfaces. Other antibodies attach to surfaces and cause clumps to form. Phagocytes then eat and destroy the clumps. Many other types of white blood cells have special tasks in the immune system.

A smoothly working immune system makes sure new cells are growing and behaving normally. Abnormal cells are immediately attacked and destroyed. This check system stops the abnormal growth of cells. Cancer is one kind of abnormal cell growth that can be stopped by this self-monitoring system.

Sometimes, the immune system needs outside help to stop abnormal cell growth. Doctors use radiation or powerful chemicals as added cancer treatment. Sometimes the immune system gets confused and starts attacking normal cells. Such illnesses are known as *autoimmune diseases.*

In the eighteenth and nineteenth centuries, doctors started using vaccines to fight infectious diseases. A vaccination is an injection of a dead or weakened virus that causes the body to produce antibodies. A vaccination does not usually make a person sick. Instead it provides protection against future infection.

Immunologist

Dr. John Finerty
National Cancer
Institute
Bethesda, Maryland

I am manager of an immunology program at the National Cancer Institute. The Cancer Institute is part of a government organization called the National Institutes of Health (NIH).

I am also the chairman of the microbiology and immunology department at the NIH Foundation for Advancement in the Education of Science. It is there that I teach a course on immunology. That's the study of the body's ability to resist infections.

Various people—scientists, physicians, technicians, patent attorneys, and high school students enrolled in precollege courses—take my course to help them with their work.

I've always been interested in biology. When I was young, we lived in Maryland near where a river empties into the Chesapeake Bay. It was a great place to explore. I could find both freshwater and saltwater clams near my house. Dissecting clams was of great interest to me.

My parents encouraged my interest in science. Unlike many of the other children in my neighborhood, I was preoccupied with exploring and reading. At the age of ten, my parents gave me a microscope. I used the microscope to look at frog blood, fish blood, and my own blood.

Insects, protozoa, and organisms attached to seaweed also fell under my eye thanks to my microscope. I liked looking at different crystal structures, too. My parents also bought me a chemistry set. In fact, our kitchen became the lab where I did my experiments.

If you want to be a scientist, read everything. Early on I read every issue of *Scientific American*. I still refer to articles from it in my immunology class.

My eighth-grade teacher, Ms. Murphy, was great. She helped keep my interest in science alive. She let me use a professional microscope. I spent many hours learning to use it and looking at various things.

In high school, I often stayed after school to use the more powerful microscopes and chemicals. It's very important that your science teachers give you plenty of hands-on experiences.

I'm involved in research on resistance to infectious diseases. I work with mice since they are easy to handle. I make vaccines to prevent them from becoming ill. Then I infect the mice to see if the vaccine works.

We know which mouse genes are resistant to infectious diseases. When we do experiments, we use knock-out mice. They are mice that have a gene inactivated in a particular part of the immune system. We infect a knock-out mouse with a disease and observe the animal. We apply the concepts learned from these experiments to humans.

During the Vietnam War, I went to the Walter Reed Army Medical Center for conferences every two weeks. One time we saw soldiers who had just returned from Vietnam. They were having a hard time breathing. They also had high fevers and low blood counts. The level of oxygen in their blood was dropping fast. Some of them were dying. These soldiers had malaria. I suggested giving the soldiers pure oxygen. It worked! It actually saved their lives!

The world will need more immunologists in the future. They will help discover new antibiotics and vaccines.

Bacteria are becoming resistant to some antibiotics. What will happen if bacteria become completely resistant? Children could die of strep throat. Tuberculosis patients would have to go back to the treatments we used before we discovered antibiotics. They will be sent to sanitariums to spend months sitting on porches where there is plenty of fresh air and sunshine. Fresh air, sunshine, rest, and good food can help tuberculosis patients fight off the disease.

Students who are interested in infectious diseases should take biology, chemistry, and computer courses. Learn how to use the Internet. The Internet is a global network of people connected via computers. Scientists use it to exchange information and to have discussions with scientists in other countries. Take a debating class too. It can help you learn how to explain your thoughts to others.

Most people don't realize they are using science in their daily lives. I use my knowledge of biology and chemistry in working with my compost heap. I throw all the kitchen garbage except meat in the compost heap. Once the compost gets going, bacteria and fungi break down the waste. I even put junk mail and cardboard boxes in it. They take about a month to decompose.

I have also been experimenting with plastic foam and plastic bottles to see if they will decompose. I use the decomposed material on my garden.

You can use science to help yourself or to improve life for other people.

DISCOVERY FILE

Lung Cancer

Cancer can grow in the lungs or in the air passages leading to the lungs. Lung cancer is very common and is strongly associated with cigarette smoking. The disease can also be caused by exposure to industrial air pollutants, such as the particles of one type of asbestos.

All cancers occur when cells begin to divide in abnormal and uncontrolled ways. These malignant cells invade and destroy surrounding tissue. Cancer can spread to other organs and tissues through the bloodstream or the lymphatic system. It can also spread within the body's hollow cavities.

Early stages of lung cancer often show no symptoms. The disease can be diagnosed by x-ray examination. During its later stages, lung cancer typically causes a persistent cough.

Surgeons often remove the diseased lung or section of lung. Surgery helps about 20 percent of cases. Other treatments include radiation and chemotherapy.

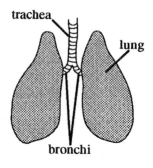

Born Fighters

Purpose

To find out how the body uses antibodies to fight disease.

Background

In epidemics, huge numbers of people get sick. Some people die, while others only get a mild form of the disease, then recover completely. Some individuals are exposed, but do not seem to get the disease at all. The reason is antibodies. Antibodies are chemicals your body makes to fight disease. If you already have antibodies against a particular disease, you are immune to that disease. If you don't have them yet, when you catch a disease, your body begins to make antibodies. Either way, antibodies can punch holes in the invading germs or cause them to clump together so that they can be eaten by white blood cells called phagocytes.

People in your community are sick. Some are dying and some are getting milder cases. Do they all have the same disease? Do some people already have antibodies against the germ?

Perhaps we can narrow down the cause of the disease by testing blood serum from some of the victims. If we test blood with a solution containing known disease germs, an antigen-antibody reaction will show that a patient has made antibodies to fight that particular germ.

You are a member of a research team from the Center for Control of Infectious Diseases (CCID). You have received serum samples from the members of one family. Three people in this family have symptoms of the disease that's going around. Your assignment is to test the serum and report your findings. This is a double-blind study. You will not be given the name of the family, nor will you be told which family members have symptoms of the disease.

Before you start, you decide to read over the procedures for testing human serum for the presence of the kind of antibodies that cause clumping. Serum is the liquid part of the blood with its clotting factors removed.

Materials

- Five labeled dropper bottles each containing serum from a different member of an infected family (labeled with identifying numbers 1 through 5)
- One dropper bottle containing a clear liquid labeled "TB germs"
- Microscope slides
- Toothpicks
- Paper towels for clean-up

Procedure

1. Plan with your research team how you will test and record the reactions of the five different serum samples. You will use the bacteria and other materials provided.
2. Set up an illustrated chart so your procedure and results can be clearly communicated to other research teams working on the same problem.

Testing for the Presence of Antibodies — Clumping

Some antibodies work by causing clumping. These antibodies have shapes that attach to features on the outside of invading organisms. Only the right shape will fit, like only the right key will open a lock. One antibody will attach to several invaders causing clumps to form.

To test for the presence of clumping antibodies in a sample of blood serum, do the following:

- Place a drop of serum on a clean microscope slide.
- Next to that drop, place a drop of solution containing a known disease-causing organism.
- Use a new toothpick or sterile instrument to carefully mix the two drops together.
- Observe for changes that indicate a clumping together of the microscopic germ particles. Positive changes may appear as visible specks or as a clouding of the liquid. These changes indicate that the serum already contains antibodies for the disease germs.
- If the drops remain clear, the test is negative. The serum does not contain antibodies for the disease germs.

---

3. Complete all tests according to your team's plan.

Conclusion A

Prepare a fax to send to your department director at the CCID. Be sure to report your results, describe your lab procedures, and state your conclusions.

After you turn in your fax, your teacher will give you a return fax. It will be from your CCID director. Review any new information it contains. If your conclusions change, prepare a new fax explaining the changes. (You may need to read the Discovery File on tuberculosis before you write your answer.)

Conclusion B

A publisher is developing a pamphlet about immunity. The audience for the pamphlet will be young children and their parents. A section in the pamphlet will be called *The Importance of Immunizations*. In addition to discussing the reasons for vaccinations, it will explain how vaccines induce immunity, and give a brief history of Edward Jenner's contribution to our knowledge about immunity. Divide the work for this section of the pamphlet among the members of your team. (You may need to read the Discovery Files on immunity and famous disease fighters before you write your answer.)

STUDENT VOICES

Everybody in my family was worried about catching Ebola. We bought our water and bought imported food. We didn't go out anymore; we stayed in.

During the outbreak, I had malaria. I thought I had Ebola. I never went outside. I just stayed in my room and took a lot of medicine.

I would never go to sleep without praying.

YOMBO MUTUMBA
ZAMBIAN
KIMSHASA, ZAIRE

Staying Well

When certain worms, fungi, bacteria, and viruses enter your body, they can cause infection or disease. The infection might be in only one part of your body, such as in a boil or sore. Infection might spread throughout your body and cause fever, aches, an increase in the number of white blood cells, a runny nose, and other symptoms.

Infectious diseases are spread in a variety of ways. Some disease-causing organisms live in water, entering your body when you drink it. Cholera is a deadly waterborne disease. It spreads when people drink water contaminated with infected feces.

Some infectious agents travel through the air. When people cough or sneeze, tiny droplets containing virus particles spray the air. The common cold is a good example of an airborne disease. Legionnaire's disease, a type of pneumonia, and chicken pox are also transmitted through the air.

Infections can enter your body through food. The deadly *Clostridium botulinum* bacterium causes botulism. It is usually found in improperly preserved meats. *Salmonella*, another food-borne bacterium, causes food poisoning and can even cause death.

A public health concern in the United States is the *Escherichia coli* bacterium that can contaminate undercooked meat. *E. coli* bacteria are found in the intestines of healthy humans and animals. However, some strains of *E. coli* cause diarrhea, severe stomach upset, and sometimes kidney failure.

Knowing how diseases spread will help you protect yourself from them. Your local sewage plant probably does a good job of protecting you from waterborne bacteria. But after floods or hurricanes, you may have to filter or boil your water for a time. On a camping trip, use a chemical or a filter to purify your water.

Good personal hygiene habits can help protect you from disease. Cover your mouth when you cough or sneeze. Dispose of paper tissues after you use them. Use your own glass, especially when you or others are sick. Be sure to wash your hands after you use the toilet. Keep yourself in good health. You are more susceptible to bacteria and viruses when you are tired or not eating properly.

Careful food handling can also help protect you. Make sure your hands are clean before handling food. Wash fruits and vegetables thoroughly to remove bacteria and insecticides. Cook meat thoroughly.

Refrigerate all foods that need to be cold and keep hot foods hot until serving them. Make sure your refrigerator temperature is in the proper range. If you do not know whether a food item is still good or has spoiled, throw it away.

Another way to protect yourself and your community from diseases is by vaccination. Doctors usually give vaccines by injection with needles. Sometimes you can take vaccines in liquid form by mouth.

In the United States, vaccinations are given to protect children from measles, mumps, rubella (German measles), diphtheria, tetanus, and polio. Many schools require proof of vaccination before enrolling a student. A vaccine for chicken pox has recently become available. Vaccinations for adults include influenza, hepatitis B, and bacterial pneumonia.

Antibiotic misuse breeds superbugs

By Anita Manning
USA TODAY

More than half of American adults who take antibiotics don't take them as prescribed, a new survey shows.

Doctors warn that such misuse is partly to blame for the evolution of superbugs — bacteria that don't respond to a widening array of drugs.

The Gallup survey, funded by Pfizer Inc., and released today by the American Lung Association, questioned 100 physicians and 1,010 others. Results:

▶ Of the 895 who had used an antibiotic, 52% didn't finish their prescription.

▶ Of those who didn't finish, 54% stopped taking the medication because they felt better; 81% didn't tell their doctors they stopped.

▶ Most physicians (72%) say their patients don't understand the difference between viral and bacterial respiratory tract infections and say on average, 7 of 10 patients ask for antibiotics to treat viral infections, such as cold or flu.

But antibiotics don't have any effect against viruses, and using the drugs inappropriately or not completing the full prescription can lead to antibiotic resistance, says Dr. Herbert Wiedemann of the Cleveland Clinic Foundation.

"If an antibiotic is prescribed for 10 days and the patient stops taking it after three or four days, that may allow for the emergence of resistant organisms," says Wiedemann.

Cutting short the treatment period or taking lower doses than prescribed kills only the most drug-sensitive bacteria, clearing the way for resistant bacteria to survive a few days' attack by antibiotics, he says.

USA TODAY, 12 OCTOBER, 1995

Hotlines for Health

Many national health organizations have toll-free telephone numbers you can call for more information. You can find local organizations and units of these national organizations in your local telephone book.

Remember, knowledge is power. Whether you want information for a research project, for yourself, for a family member, or for a friend, these organizations are set up to help you.

AIDS (Acquired Immunodeficiency Syndrome)
- U.S. Public Health Service: 1-800-342-AIDS
- Teen AIDS Information: 1-800-234-TEEN

Alcohol
- National Council on Alcoholism: 1-800-NCA-CALL

Allergies
- American Academy of Allergy & Immunology: 1-800-822-2762

Alzheimer's disease
- Alzheimer's Disease and Related Disorders Association: 1-800-621-0379

Anorexia/bulimia
- Bulimia Anorexia Self-Help: 1-800-BASH-STL

Arthritis
- Arthritis Foundation: 1-800-283-7800

Asthma
- National Asthma Center: 1-800-222-5864

Cancer
- American Cancer Society: 1-800-ACS-2345
- National Cancer Institute: 1-800-4-CANCER

Diabetes
- American Diabetes Foundation: 1-800-232-3472
- Juvenile Diabetes Foundation: 1-800-223-1138

Domestic violence
- National Domestic Violence Hotline: 1-800-333-SAFE

Drug abuse
- Just Say No Clubs: 1-800-258-2766
- National Institute on Drug Abuse: 1-800-662-HELP

Dyslexia
- Orton Dyslexia Society: 1-800-ABCD-123

Epilepsy
- Epilepsy Foundation of America: 1-800-332-1000

Heart
- American Heart Association: 1-800-242-8721

Lung diseases
- American Lung Association: no national 800 number; check local listings

Death toll from infectious diseases increases

By Anita Manning
USA TODAY

Infectious diseases, once thought to be nearly vanquished by modern medicine, are on the rise in the U.S., say federal health officials.

The rate of deaths caused by such illnesses grew 58%, from 41 to 65 deaths per 100,000 between 1980 and 1992, says a report based on a study of death certificates.

"Infectious diseases had declined dramatically in the U.S." earlier this century, says Dr. Robert W. Pinner of the Centers for Disease Control and Prevention, whose report is in today's *Journal of the American Medical Association.* That trend was expected to continue, he says, but "the events of the last few years demonstrate infectious diseases continue to play havoc."

Some of the increase can be explained. Respiratory tract infections, which occur primarily in older people, caused 47% of infectious disease deaths in 1992. When figures were adjusted for age, infectious disease deaths increased 39%.

Another factor is the emergence of HIV. When HIV deaths are subtracted from the study, the increase in infectious disease deaths was 22%.

In 1980, infectious disease was the fifth-leading cause of death, but by 1992 it had moved to the third spot, after heart disease and cancer, the researchers write. "We don't have a full explanation for these increases," says Pinner.

USA TODAY, 17 JANUARY, 1996

Social Studies: Where in the World is Sao Paulo-A?

Purpose
To complete an unfinished story about a fictitious disease, accounting for its spread over three different continents.

Materials
For each student or group:
- Small map of the world (desk size)
- Atlas
- Reference books
- Markers

Background
The Centers for Disease Control (CDC) released a report about a new virus spreading throughout the world. Originally thought to be dangerous, the virus (which scientists named Sao Paulo-A) turns out to be short-lived and relatively harmless.

Symptoms of Sao Paulo-A are unpleasant, but never life threatening. The virus first causes a mild fever. Next, a mild rash appears on the upper body. Some victims feel nauseated. Symptoms disappear after three days.

After much research into the Sao Paulo-A virus, scientists discovered it can be spread through casual contact. Hand-shakes, coughs, or shared food can spread the virus, although only some people who come in contact with the virus actually become sick from it.

The virus has an incubation period of 14 days. In other words, 14 days after a person is exposed, symptoms begin to appear. Also, for the last seven days of the incubation period and for the three days of the disease, infected people are contagious and can spread Sao Paulo-A.

Procedure
The CDC's report (opposite) profiles three early carriers of Sao Paulo-A.
1. Create and write a scenario for the fourth carrier. Use the fourth carrier to show the spread of Sao Paulo-A to at least three different continents using at least three different modes of transportation.
2. Use an atlas or other reference to find reasons for people to be traveling among the different countries. Research exports and imports for the countries you use. Note methods of transport so your scenario will be realistic. An outstanding scenario will have at least five travelers going to at least three different continents by a variety of travel methods. All traveling should be realistic and based on your research.
3. Be careful to spread the disease from person to person only during its contagious period. Timing is crucial.

Conclusion
1. Once you have written the fourth scenario, make a diagram or chart that shows everyone each person contacted. Include each city, how long the disease took to reach each city, and how it got there. The chart must be clearly organized, neat, and easily understood.
2. On a map of the world, use arrows to show the spread of Sao Paulo-A based on the four different scenarios. Make each of the four scenarios visually different from the others. Use a key to explain what the map shows.

REPORT FROM THE CENTERS FOR DISEASE CONTROL
THE SPREAD OF SAO PAULO-A

Evidence suggests that Sao Paulo-A began in the Amazon rain forest. Its first appearance in a heavily-populated area has been traced to Sao Paulo, Brazil.

At an international soccer match between Brazil and Germany, four people shared a luxury box. The waiter who served them had recently arrived in Sao Paulo from a small village near the confluence of the Negro and Amazon rivers.

Tests show that the blood of all inhabitants of that village contains antibodies to the Sao Paulo-A virus. However, no one in the village has had any of the symptoms.

Two weeks after the soccer game, all four people in the luxury box came down with Sao Paulo-A symptoms.

The Ambassador

The German Ambassador to Brazil purchased the luxury box for the soccer match. He had three guests in the box.

A week after the soccer game, the ambassador returned to Germany to lecture at the University of Frankfurt. A student from Ankara, Turkey, picked him up at the airport. The student accompanied the ambassador during his two-day stay in Frankfurt.

Eight days after the ambassador's departure, the student flew to Ankara to visit his family.

In Ankara, he met an old friend who was now a truck driver. The two had dinner one evening, then went to a movie. The next day, the driver left Ankara with a load of automobile batteries for Cairo, Egypt. The trip took five days.

He stayed in Cairo for another four days waiting to pick up a return cargo. While waiting, the driver stayed at a small hotel owned by a Moslem family. He saw members of the family each day as they serviced his room and prepared his meals in the hotel's small restaurant.

One week after the driver left, the Moslem family left on a pilgrimage, or *Hadj*, to Mecca. In Mecca, they stayed in a hostel with other Moslems from all over the world. The ambassador, the Turkish student, the driver, the Moslem family, and the hosteler all displayed symptoms of Sao Paulo-A.

The Mine Owner

One of the ambassador's guests at the game was an Australian mine owner. She was in Brazil looking for new mining opportunities for her company.

She left two days after the game to take a nine-day cruise to Australia. Upon reaching Sydney, the owner met with her staff and her personal secretary.

That night, the secretary returned home to her husband, who is the first mate on a bulk-cargo ship. He left four days later carrying wheat to Singapore.

The first mate went shopping in Singapore to buy a gift for his wife. While in a department store, he met the store's buyer.

A week later, the buyer went to Shanghai to search for new sources of goods for the department store. While in Shanghai, the buyer met with his cousin, who was an entrepreneur.

The cousin took a boat up the Yangtze River to Chongqing where he met with a factory manager. The mine owner, her secretary, the first mate, the buyer, the cousin, and the factory manager all eventually displayed signs of Sao Paulo-A.

The Oil Broker

The ambassador's second guest in the box was an oil broker from Venezuela. After the game, she returned immediately to Caracas.

Eight days later, she inspected one of her tankers as it was preparing to deliver a load of oil to Havana, Cuba. The oil broker shook hands with the ship's captain and kissed him good-bye on both cheeks.

Seven days later, after a few other stops, the tanker docked in Havana. The captain shook hands and hugged his old friend the harbormaster.

Twelve days later, the harbormaster and his family escaped from Cuba in a friend's boat. Once in Miami, the family moved in with relatives who had immigrated there several years before.

One of the relatives worked as a clerk at a Miami resort. Thirteen days after the harbormaster's family arrived from Cuba, this clerk waited on a tourist from New Orleans.

The tourist left Miami and drove back to New Orleans. She visited her mother in New Orleans two days later.

Eleven days passed, then her mother left on a steamboat up the Mississippi River to St. Louis to visit her sister. The oil broker, the captain, the harbormaster, the clerk, the tourist, the mother, and the sister all eventually displayed signs of Sao Paulo-A.

Math: Warm-Up Activities

Purpose
To practice math skills using scenarios about infectious diseases.

Background
When health officials, scientists, or others investigate and cure infectious diseases, they often use mathematics. For example, if 12 people in your community are infected with the flu, and if each one infects 2 other people, how many people now have the flu?

Procedure
Do the following warm-up activities as directed by your teacher:

1. If the health department recommends a 0.05 g dose of antibiotic for each person each week as a preventative, how many grams of antibiotic must be purchased to treat 100,000 people a week for four weeks? How many kilograms?

2. If 125 people visited the Second Street Medical Center every 30 minutes, how many hours would it take to treat 10,000 people?

3. There are 72 known cases of an infectious disease at Central Middle School. Central Middle School has an enrollment of 960 students. What is the probability that a randomly selected student at Central Middle School has the disease? Express your answer as a fraction, a decimal, and a percent.

4. When the school nurse made a presentation in your class, he advised you to avoid shaking each other's hands. He made his point by telling the class that if each of the 21 students on bus number 124 shook each other's hands, there would be 105 handshakes. Is he right? Show how many handshakes there would be. Does your answer help make the nurse's point?

5. Your doctor has given you preventive medicine that you must take at least 2 hours and 45 minutes before being around other people. What is the latest time you could take the medicine before attending a dance that begins at 7:30 p.m.?

6. A new bacterial disease has been discovered. When in a human body at 98.6° F, its number doubles every 20 minutes. In how many hours will a single cell reach the 1,000,000 cells required to make a person nauseous?

Math: Predicting the Casualties

Purpose
To investigate the rapid growth of a single-cell organism and to calculate the impact of an epidemic on a community.

Materials
For each student:
- Several sheets of chart or grid paper
- Computer with spreadsheet software
- Calculator

Background
People in the city are just becoming aware of the chronic illness spreading through the area. This morning's newspaper reported that 100,000 people are now affected; the number is increasing rapidly.

The Board of Health wants you to make a table that shows the growth of a single bacterium. They also want you to estimate the number of community members who will be affected by the time researchers develop a cure.

Cases are currently increasing at the rate of 12 percent per month. Researchers estimate they need two more years to find a cure. If no action is taken, the 12-percent increase will continue.

Health officials have developed two plans to slow the advance of the epidemic. Experience in other communities suggests that an educational program may save 1,000 people per month. The second plan involves providing massive doses of preventative medicines to slow the epidemic advance to 8 percent per month.

Procedure
1. Chart the growth of a bacterium that reproduces by simple cell division once every 20 minutes.
2. Make a table and a graph showing the number of organisms created during a 3-hour period. Use $C = 2^t$ where C is the number of cells and t is the number of 20-minute time periods.
3. How many people will become infected before a cure is found? To make your estimate, use a computer with a spreadsheet program. Create a column in which you begin with the starting figure of 10,000 then multiply it in the cell below by 1.12. This represents a 12-percent increase. Copy that cell down the column to represent 24 months (the estimated time it will take for a cure to be found).
4. How many people will become infected if the educational campaign is used? To make your estimate, use a computer with a spreadsheet program. Create another column in which you begin with the starting figure of 10,000 then multiply it in the cell below by 1.12 and subtract 1000. This represents a 12-percent increase minus 1000. Copy that cell down the column to represent 24 months.
5. How many people will become infected if preventative medicines are used? To make your estimate, use a computer with a spreadsheet program. Create another column in which you begin with the starting figure of 10,000 then multiply it in the cell below by 1.08. This represents an 8-percent increase. Copy that cell down the column to represent 24 months.
6. Design and construct a table and a graph showing the number of people infected in one year under these three scenarios:
   - take no action
   - conduct educational campaign
   - provide preventative medicines
7. The federal government will assist when the number of affected people reaches 500,000. At what point will the federal government get involved under each plan?

Conclusion
Make a recommendation to the Board of Health for immediate action. Hurry! If you wait until tomorrow, the data will change! You can choose from the choices presented or you can come up with a plan that involves a combination of all or parts of the plans. If you invent a new plan, try to develop a new column on your spreadsheet that demonstrates how your new plan improves the numbers.

Writing: A Contest

Purpose
To produce a brochure about a disease caused by a pathogenic organism.

Materials
- References about disease-causing organisms
- Colored paper
- Colored pencils or markers

Background
PILLCo is a pharmaceutical company in your community. They are sponsoring a contest for middle school students. The contest asks students to produce a three-panel brochure about one kind of organism that causes infectious diseases. Photos of the first, second, and third place winners will be printed in the local newspaper.

PILLCo hopes that by sponsoring this contest, they will inform the public about diseases and about PILLCo products. (PILLCo develops vaccines and treatments for infectious diseases.)

PILLCo's president also hopes to demonstrate that the company cares about the young people of the community.

Your school has decided to compete.

Procedure
The rules say each brochure must have an accurate, labeled diagram of one of the following causes of disease:
1. Virus
2. Bacterium
3. Fungus
4. Protozoan
5. Parasitic worm

The brochure must also include the names of several diseases caused by that kind of organism. Include a description of the symptoms, prevention, treatment, and cure of each disease.

Conclusions
1. Explain a draft of your brochure to at least two other students. Use a copy of the Peer-Response Form on page 53. Encourage constructive criticisms. Based on this peer review, correct and improve your brochure.
2. Work with your class to create a rubric for the judges to use.
3. Pretend you are a judge. Use the class rubric to judge five entries. Submit your findings to PILLCo's public relations manager (your teacher). After this, the class will determine a winner and runners up.

Peer-Response Form

Directions

1. Ask your partners to listen carefully as you read your rough draft aloud.

2. Ask your partners to help you improve your writing by telling you their answers to the questions below.

3. Jot down notes about what your partners say:

   a. What did you like best about my rough draft?

   b. What did you have the hardest time understanding in my rough draft?

   c. What can you suggest that I do to improve my rough draft?

4. Exchange rough drafts with a partner. In pencil, place a check mark near any mechanical, spelling, punctuation, or grammatical constructions about which you are uncertain. Return the papers and check your own. Ask your partner for clarification if you do not understand or agree with the comments on your paper. Jot down notes you want to remember when writing your revision.

Proofreading Guidesheet

1. Have you identified the assigned purpose of the writing assignment? Have you accomplished this purpose?

2. Have you written on the assigned topic?

3. Have you identified the assigned form your writing should take? Have you written accordingly?

4. Have you addressed the assigned audience in your writing?

5. Have you used sentences of different lengths and types to make your writing effective?

6. Have you chosen language carefully so the reader understands what you mean?

7. Have you done the following to make your writing clear for someone else to read?

   - used appropriate capitalization
   - kept pronouns clear
   - kept verb tense consistent
   - used correct spelling
   - used correct punctuation
   - used complete sentences
   - made all subjects and verbs agree
   - organized your ideas into logical paragraphs

Acknowledgments

Author
Russell G. Wright, with contributions from Leonard David, Barbara Sprungman, Janet Wert Crampton, and the following teachers:

Science Activities
*Barbara L. Teichman, Parkland Middle School, Rockville, MD
*Frank S. Weisel, Tilden Middle School, North Bethesda, MD

Teacher Advisors
*Patricia L. Berard, Colonel E. Brooke Lee Middle School, Silver Spring, MD
*William R. Krayer, Gaithersburg High School, Gaithersburg, MD
*Henry Milne, Cabin John Middle School, Potomac, MD
*Eugene M. Molesky, Ridgeview Middle School, Gaithersburg, MD
*Kenneth A. Schmidt, Redland Middle School, Rockville, MD

Interdisciplinary Activities
*James J. Deligianis, Tilden Middle School, North Bethesda, MD
*Cuyler J. Cornell, Cabin John Middle School, Potomac, MD

Event-Site Support
Tracy Wright, The American School of Kinshasa, Kinshasa, Zaire

Scientific Review
Jonathan Smith, U.S. Army Research Institute for Infectous Diseases, Fort Detrick, MD
John F. Finerty, National Cancer Institute, Bethesda, MD
Susan Smythers, Montgomery County Department of Health and Human Services, Silver Spring, MD

*Asterisks indicate Montgomery County Schools

Student Consultants
*Parkland Middle School, Rockville, MD:
Becky White, Anna Burrows, Paul DiBlasi, Dariush Samari, Gueck Lim, Terri Prather, Curtis Jones, Alfonso Diaz
*Ridgeview Middle School, Gaithersburg, MD:
Nikhil Nagendran, Siddharth Nagendran, Bryan Peacock
*Robert Frost Middle School, Rockville, MD:
Theodore Deligianis

Field-Test Teachers
Patricia Flynn, Agawam Jr. High, Feeding Hills, MA
Cheryl Glotfelty and Linda Mosser, Northern Middle School, Accident, MD
Gerry Harrison, Sevier Middle School, Kingsport, TN
Hope Hall, Ross N. Robinson Middle School, Kingsport, TN
Lilla Green, Hartigan School, Chicago, IL
Judy Kidd, South Charlotte Middle School, Charlotte, NC
Helen Linn and Cathy Miller, Huron Middle School, Northglenn, CO
Wendy Beavis and Mike Geil, Tanana Middle School, Fairbanks, AK

EBS Advisory Committee
Dr. Joseph Antensen, Baltimore City Public Schools
Ms. Deanna Banks-Beane, Association of Science-Technology Centers
Ms. MaryAnn Brearton, American Association for the Advancement of Science
Dr. Jack Cairns, Delaware Dept. of Public Instruction
Mr. Bob Dubill, USA Today
Mr. Gary Heath, Maryland State Department of Education
Dr. Henry Heikkinen, University of Northern Colorado
Dr. Ramon Lopez, American Physical Society
Dr. J. David Lockard, University of Maryland (Emeritus)
Dr. Wayne A. Moyer, Montgomery County Public Schools (Retired)
Dr. Arthur Popper, University of Maryland